BIZA
BRIGHTON

To Russell, very best
wishes
Chris Horlock

Christopher Horlock

Dedication

This book is dedicated to my two wonderful children, Charlotte and George, who aren't in the slightest phased by weird and wonderful things; in fact they probably like them more than I do.

First published in 2010 by S B Publications
Tel: 01323 893498
Email: *sbpublications@tiscali.co.uk*
Website: *www.sbpublications.co.uk*

ISBN 978-185770-3511

Layout by Vital Signs Publishing
Email: *info@vitalsignspublishing.co.uk*

Acknowledgements

I have to thank Robert Jeeves of Step Back In Time, Queen's Road in Brighton, for allowing some of his celebrated postcards to be used in the book (e.g. the 'bullet in the bible' picture, the Court Theatre, etc.) and Alan Hayes let me use his Brighton Festival 'painting the sea' pictures. The photo of Henry Holden's grave was given to me quite a while ago and I've lost track of who the donor was – so thanks to them whoever they were! Virtually all the other pictures are from my own collection. One or two are really old photographs or drawings for which it's been impossible to determine ownership. I hope I haven't infringed anyone's copyright by including them. My talented daughter, Charlotte, drew the picture of James Ings on page 11 and took the picture of me, page 82.

I have to thank big brother, Stephen Horlock, head of all the cemeteries in Brighton and Hove, and his right-hand man, Alan Virgo, for tracking down several graves and even photographing them for me, which was well beyond the call of duty and saved me a lot of legwork!

I acknowledge using David Rowland's book The Brighton Blitz as the source for wartime bombing facts and figures, Douglas d'Enno's Brighton Crime and Vice 1800 – 2000 for some of the crime information – plus a picture or two - and the late David Adland's Brighton's Music Halls for the story of illusionist Ling Look - The Great Chinese Salamander.

But most of all, I have to thank all the people who have told me strange things about Brighton and Hove over the years, mostly 'old timers', including Antony Dale, James Gray, Cliff Edwards, fisherman Jim Sinden (a relation of Donald Sinden, the actor) and John Barrow, sadly all now departed. There have been many others. Their tales live on!

Contents

Author's introduction

Where to start with all the strange stories and weird snippets of information I've unearthed or have been told over the years about Brighton and Hove? And where to end? It's been a hard job deciding which to include and which to leave out. Some, of course – the well-known ones that most people have heard of - just had to be re-related, so the outrageous behaviour of the Prince of Wales and his friends the Barrys, plus silly goings on at the Pavilion, are all here, as are Brighton 'immortals' Sake Deen Mahomed, the Green Man and Phoebe Hessell, plus some familiar ghostly tales, wartime bombing incidents and brilliant hoaxes.

But others appear for the first time. Who would have thought that rabbits and hares (even just mentioning them) would have caused such dread and horror amongst Brighton's fishing community? Did artist van Gogh really visit Brighton? Why was a wall built – in Robert Street – with nine skulls embedded in it? And how was it that wives (yes, married women!) were for sale at Brighton's market in the early 1800s?

In the end I went for a broad mix of stories and anecdotes, ranging from the deadly serious, to the highly silly, from the well known to the completely unknown. And as well as being thoroughly quirky they had to be entertaining stories that would either raise a smile, lift eyebrows in disbelief or generate a shudder of horror. I really hope it's a satisfying mix. I know those who do walking tours of Brighton, particularly during the three-week Festival in May, are going to seize on some of the stories here and recount them as they take people around the city on historic walks or 'ghost trails'. I hope, too, that even those who know the history of Brighton and Hove really well will find something new in these pages.

CHRISTOPHER HORLOCK

1: Bizarre people, or fairly ordinary people who have done bizarre things

Brighton has always been famed for its celebrities and colourful characters, so what follow are short accounts of who some were and what they did. Several are well known – some definitely not (until now that is!)

Anthony Stapley

This gentleman would be top in the group of famous 'stroppy' Brightonians from the past – and there have been many!

Actually, he wasn't a Brighton man, but was born at Framfield, near Uckfield, and owned several Sussex properties including Patcham Place, still with us, a large house off the London Road, and today a youth hostel - that's the Brighton connection. Stapley was an MP for New Shoreham and later for Lewes, then became Governor of Chichester from 1643-1645.

During the Civil War of the 1640s – where King Charles I battled with Parliament over who ultimately ruled the nation - Sussex was divided in its loyalties. Some areas were fiercely Royalist, others supported Parliament's champion, Oliver Cromwell. Brighton seemed definitely the latter. Stapley – at first a general in Cromwell's 'New Model Army' - was obviously a staunch Parliamentarian and became one of the fifty-nine regicides who actually signed Charles' death warrant, which led to the king's execution in January 1649 and the end of royal rule. It doesn't get much stroppier than that! Stapley died in 1655 (he's buried at Patcham), so missed all the really nasty repercussions meted out to the regicides when Charles' son was restored to the throne five years later. Stapley is said to haunt Patcham House.

Patcham House

Phoebe Hessell

Phoebe Hessell's grave is in St Nicholas' churchyard, just up from the Clock Tower, and shows she was born in Stepney in April 1713 and died in Brighton, at the great age of 108, in December 1821. Hessel Street and Amazon Street in London – she was nicknamed 'the Amazon of Stepney' – are named after her. The story making her a legendary Brighton celebrity is well known, but goes as follows. When a young woman, she fell in love with a soldier named Sam Golding, who found himself posted to the West Indies. She decided to follow him by joining the same regiment – the 5th Foot - disguised as a man.

Phoebe Hessell in old age

She kept up the pretence well enough to serve with him at the Battle of Fontenoy in Belgium in 1745 (where Britain and her allies were fighting against the French) and, having survived that, was moved along with Sam to Gibraltar. Here she was badly wounded and had to reveal who she was to the wife of the regiment's General. She was sent back to England, eventually married Sam, and they had nine children, although eight died in infancy. Sam died after twenty years of marriage and she then wed a Brighton fisherman. He died in 1792 and she took to the pubs telling her story to anyone who would stand her a drink and a pie. She could often be seen in Old Steine, selling trinkets, pin cushions and gingerbread from a basket.

At sometime she was pointed out to the Prince of Wales (the future George IV of course). He discovered she'd fallen on hard times, being forced into the workhouse in her nineties. In 1808, he granted a pension of half a guinea a week and, though now 95, she took to the streets again to sell her wares. In 1820, when George succeeded to the throne, he invited Phoebe to his coronation parade in Brighton. She died the following year – a Brighton celebrity.

Phoebe Hessell's grave

Great story though this is, it was discredited in 1972 by the research of Charles Collinson of Worthing. The 5th Foot weren't even at the Battle of Fontenoy (they had been posted to Ireland) and even if she had been there, she couldn't have confessed her identity to the General's wife because he'd left the regiment – his wife with him - in 1732!

Old legends die hard and the successors of the 5th Foot won't have her story any other way than how she told it. They're now the Northumberland Fusiliers and still pay for the upkeep of her grave. Her portrait hangs in their mess HQ and, to them, she's still their great hero (well, heroine!).

The Chevalier d'Eon

Truly a deliciously bizarre moment in Brighton's history took place in 1793. At this time, the Theatre Royal in New Road didn't exist ; the town's theatre was then in Duke Street, about halfway down the northern side. An extremely skilful fencer, named the Chevalier D'Eon, appeared here with a display of fancy swordsmanship, performing tricks and ending his act by taking on someone from the audience. Nothing very sensational about that, at this time anyway, only what was unusual was he did his act dressed as a woman. Was he the first example of 'drag' on

The Duke Street Theatre

a public stage in Britain? He certainly seems a first for Brighton. 'All the world wondered,' we read, 'whether the fencer was man or woman. Curiosity to see 'the lady' was wrought up to the highest pitch; and never was there such excitement at the theatre since it had been opened.'

The 'Chevalier' was, in reality, totally male and had worked as a spy for both Louis XV and Louis XVI (briefly), pulling off some influential diplomatic coups and generally being very useful indeed to the French government. And he was never really 'found out', even when sat next to the famous Casanova at a dinner in 1764. The notorious womaniser believed d'Eon to be 'une belle femme' as 'his voice is too clear for that of a castrato and the shape too rounded for a man'.

But such was the feverish debate about d'Eon's gender that by the 1780s a betting pool operated at the London Stock Exchange on whether he was a male or a female, with the latest odds posted in all the best coffee houses. One financier offered him £30,000 to disrobe - he didn't.

By 1785, with his sex never really confirmed one way or the other, he'd 'retired' to England and became a keen collector of books and manuscripts. MP Horace Walpole met d'Eon in 1786 and described 'her' as 'loud, noisy and vulgar – her hands and arms seem not to have participated in the change of sexes, but are fitter to carry a chair than a fan.' James

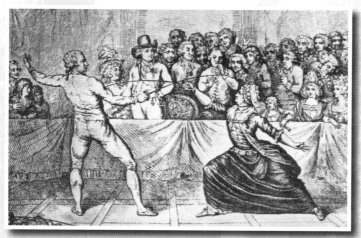

Boswell, the biographer of Samuel Johnson, wrote: 'she appeared to me a man in woman's clothes.'

To earn money, he toured with his fencing act and often participated in tournaments, fighting several times for our old friend the Prince of Wales. In 1796, three years after his appearance in Brighton, he was seriously wounded and had to 'retire' again.

The Chevalier d'Eon in action – 'she's' on the right

He died in May 1810 aged 81. A post-mortem revealed that he was definitely not a woman, nor a hermaphrodite either (as some supposed), but 100% male. Twelve witnesses at the inquest confirmed this - they found 'the male organs in every respect perfectly formed'.

George Westphal

We drift into Hove for our next famous person. The bicentenary of the Battle of Trafalgar was celebrated in 2005. Nelson's famous naval engagement of October 1805 fought off Spain, foiling Napoleon's plans to invade Britain by sea, and the Battle of Waterloo, ten years later, checked him on land. Many Sussex men took part in both campaigns.

George Westphal, a young midshipman on the Victory at Trafalgar, was present when Nelson died. Westphal had been wounded at the same time as Nelson and somehow received Nelson's coat, rolled up, under his head as a makeshift pillow. Clearly, practicalities outweighed rank! The fringe hanging from the epaulette on one shoulder caught in

George Westphal's memorial

Westphal's hair and got so tangled up it had to be cut off. He kept it, naturally, as a prized souvenir of the battle and the great admiral he served under. Westphal's subsequent career saw him knighted and achieving the rank of Admiral, and he lived – for some forty years – at no. 2 Brunswick Square, Hove. He's buried at Hove, in St Andrew's churchyard, off New Church Road.

James Ings

This old sketch of Brighton's West Street shows a shop (left) once occupied by a butcher named James Ings, another individual we can put on the list of stroppy Brightonians from the past. His shop was near the top, between North Street and Duke Street (one source says it was in Cranbourne Street, just opposite).

James Ings' shop in West Street

Cutting a long and involved story short, on 23rd February 1820, he and a number of others met up at a house in Cato Street, Paddington, planning to break into 58 Grosvenor Square that same evening and kill several prominent members of cabinet dining with the Earl of Harrowby. These men formed the core of a radical group trying to bring down the government on a number of issues, including high taxes, lack of representation and unemployment. It seems Ings, armed with his largest butcher's knife, was going to lead the storming of the house, after a kind of early hand grenade had been lobbed through an appropriate window. But the group were betrayed by informers and arrested, their plan becoming known as the Cato Street Conspiracy. Victims of a devious government set-up, all were found guilty of high treason and Ings was hanged and beheaded at Newgate prison three months later. On the scaffold, apparently, before being hanged, he started loudly singing a song called *Death or Liberty*, but one of his companions told him; 'Be quiet, Ings; we can die without all this noise.'

James Ings

There's a postscript to this story. The executioner at Newgate, who hanged Ings and the others, came from Brighton. And by the way, he didn't cut off their heads – a masked surgeon did that. He was James Botting (known as 'Jemmy') who lived in a squalid backstreet between West Street and Cannon Place, in an area now occupied by the Metropole Hotel.

The largest crowd he 'performed' for while at Newgate (he worked at other prisons too) was at the public hanging of – would you believe it – a Brighton fraudster known as James Fauntleroy, who was actually, by profession, a banker. Here the crowd was estimated to be 100,000 people. Fauntleroy's story isn't really bizarre enough to be included in this book though - it's just pretty straightforward fiddling!

Bottting became a cripple in later life and frequented the Half Moon pub in West Street, at the corner of Boyce's Street. He's said to have died when he fell out of his wheelchair and nobody came to his assistance.

It's a small Brighton (under)world isn't it?

Henry Cope - 'The Green Man'

Henry Cope

During Georgian times, many strange and eccentric people could be found in the Old Steine area, the most well known being 'The Green Man.' His real name was Henry Cope, a small man who dressed entirely in green and rode around in a green carriage. The rooms of his home were painted green and, in an age when no-one had heard the word 'vegetarian', Cope only ate fruit and green vegetables.

A Metropolitan Journal of August 1806 reported –

'Mr Cope, at four o'clock, walked on the Steyne; he wore a huge cocked hat, with gold tassels. He was surrounded with company, who expressed their surprise at the size of his hat; when he answered that he was then performing a different character from that of the preceding day. He is the gaze of Brighton. An artist yesterday took a sketch of Brighton, and intends making him and Martha Gunn the prominent figures on the canvas.'

Not a lot more is known about the Green Man, but in 1806, having become deranged even more than usual, he threw himself off the seafront cliff. Somehow he survived, and was taken to London to be looked after by friends, but we later hear a straightjacket had to be used to restrain him - was he allowed a green one we wonder?

A witty, but somewhat snide little rhyme was made up about the Green Man:

A spruce little man in a doublet of green,
Perambulates daily the streets and the Steyne,
Green striped is his waistcoat, his small clothes are green,
And oft round his neck a green 'kerchief is seen.

Green watch string, green seals, and for certain I've heard,
(Tho' they're powdered) green whiskers and eke a green beard;

Green garters, green hose, and deny it who can,
The brains too are green of this little green man!

For many years, Henry Cope's family owned a large mansion in Hartley Wintney, Hampshire, known as Bramshill. This is now the National Police Library and supposedly one of the most haunted buildings in England and includes 'The Green Man' on its list of a dozen resident ghosts. When Cope died he was wearing brown hessian boots and it's said that when his ghost appears these are, for some unaccountable reason, transparent.

Sake Deen Mahomed

A fascinating and audacious character of the Regency period – and beyond - was an Indian named Sake Deen Mahomed, who worked as a 'shampooing surgeon' in premises on the seafront, where the Queen's Hotel stands today.

About 1815, he introduced what was then a revolutionary health treatment to Brighton; for 'shampooing' under Sake Deen didn't mean a simple hair wash. It meant an extremely vigorous massage following a long 'pickling' session in a scented Turkish bath.

The initial steam bath was to make the 'patient' sweat profusely. Next, they would be encased in a flannel, tent-like garment, which had internal sleeves so an attendant could reach in and pummel and knead about at the place needing attention and keep going until some sort of relief was brought about.

Sake Deen Mahomed

Sake Deen couldn't have picked a better time to come to Brighton and set up a novel 'cure' of this kind. For 1815 was the time when the Prince Regent, heir to the throne of England, was resident in Brighton and his home, the Marine Pavilion, was about to evolve into the Royal Pavilion we see today. The town was full to overflowing with wealthy, fashionable visitors who had come for the 'sea-water cure' and enjoy the pleasures of the town's racecourse, theatre and ballrooms. Many had ailments of one sort or another they hoped sea bathing would relieve or even heal completely and if the waters didn't help, perhaps this strange new Indian's methods might just do the trick.

'A dingy new empiric has invented a new system of humbug, which is in great dispute here and is called Shampooing, a sort of stewing alive by steam,' sneered one Bernard Blackmantle, in a magazine called *The English Spy*. 'You are stabbed all the while with pads of flannels through holes in the wet blankets that surround you, until the cartilaginous substances of your joints are made as pliable as the ligaments of boiled calves' feet.'

Sake Deen's Baths

This 'humbug' treatment was, admittedly, slow to catch on with fashionable visitors, but following a few free sessions, plus claims that he could 'cure' asthma, sciatica, lumbago, paralysis, most rheumatic diseases and even loss of voice, Sake Deen's array of clients built up steadily, with patronage eventually coming from the Prince Regent no less (who we'll meet a little later on), who ordered Sake Deen to set up one of his vapour baths in the Royal Pavilion. With further assurances that even 'rejuvenation' could be brought about using his methods, his success – and wealth - was assured.

Mahomed was a native of Patna, the capital of the Bihar region of Pakistan. Born in 1759, he studied surgery at Calcutta and subsequently entered military service with the East India Company as a doctor. In 1784 he left and came to Europe, finding a wife, Jane Daly, in Cork, Ireland, with whom he eloped due to her parents' misgivings about their marriage.

The couple set up a coffee house in London in 1810, but were declared bankrupt in 1812. They next came to Brighton, where Mahomed found work as a bath house manager. Seeing the fanatical demand for restorative baths among visitors to the town, Sake Deen was quick to spot the potential for some kind of novel alternative. He acquired premises on the seafront, where King's Road joins East Street, and the words 'shampooing baths' were soon catching the eye of those promenading along the seafront.

The entrance hall to Sake Deen's baths eventually resembled a Lourdes' shrine, with discarded crutches, artificial limbs, leg irons, support corsets, neck braces and so on, festooning the walls, plus testimonials and letters on show from grateful patients who had been completely cured of their afflictions following treatment at Sake Deen's premises.

His clientele would still include the Prince when he became King George IV in 1820. George became enormously fat and pretty immobile during his reign and had to have a crane fitted alongside his steam bath, so that he could be lowered into it and hoisted out again.

The 'Royal Appointment' continued with William IV, the next king, who ruled until 1837. Prime Ministers Sir Robert Peel and Lord Canning would also feature on Sake Deen's list of satisfied customers. Occasionally someone famous, who had never suffered a day's illness in their lives, would find their name among the list of personalities cured of some horrific condition by Sake Deen, when they'd never even met the man or set foot inside his bathing establishment!

It can't have all been humbug, as Dr. John Gibney, senior Physician at Brighton's Royal Sussex County Hospital, sent patients to Sake Deen and would later write two books on bathing, the second being specifically about the benefits of vapour baths, describing Sake Deen's premises and methods in great detail.

A number of poems also appeared extolling not only Sake Deen's curative abilities but also how his success was – supposedly – bringing about the whole expansion of Brighton:

While thus beneath thy flannel shades
Fat dowagers and wrinkled maids
Re-blown in adolescence,
I marvel not that friends tell friends,
And Brighton every day extends
Its circuses and crescents

Sake Deen's grave

Sake Deen was a shrewd self-publicist and his own health was a great advertisement for his methods. He enjoyed robust fitness into advanced old age, dying in 1851. His actual age is disputed. He was probably ninety-two, but his gravestone claims he was 101. He's buried in St Nicholas' churchyard, although his grave is behind the church and can be seen, but not approached, due to a locked gate.

Mahomed's son, Arthur Akhbar Mahomed, carried on the business, not as a 'Shampooing Surgeon' but as 'Professional and Medical Rubber.'

Sake Deen himself has entered Brighton folklore as one of its most enduring characters. The 1996 Regency novel, *Lord Ramsay's Return*, was largely set in Brighton and has its heroine, Prudence Stanhope, visiting Sake Deen's premises. Sake Deen himself would have loved featuring in a novel like this – and no doubt he'd have had signed copies for sale from a stall in the foyer of his baths.

George IV and Mrs Fitzherbert

In the whole history of Brighton and Hove, no bizarre behaviour can begin to compare with that of George, Prince of Wales - builder of the Royal Pavilion, later King George IV – who had two wives at the same time, one really for business, the other pleasure, as you'll see, and this while King of England and head of the nation's church! There's no avoiding the extraordinary affairs the man got up to in a book like this, and every single thing that follows is true!

George first met the woman who was to become the love of his life – well, for most of it - at a London theatre in the 1780s. This was twenty-eight year-old Maria Fitzherbert. She was twice a widower; her first husband was killed when he fell off his horse, the second died from a chill. Charming, sophisticated and beautiful, she utterly dazzled the Prince, who was just twenty-two years old.

But he didn't exactly dazzle her, and his actions, to win her love, were a bit over the top to say the least. He spent thousands of pounds on gifts and jewellery and even feigned suicide - declaring he couldn't live without her - by stabbing (well, slightly pricking) himself and making it look far worse by squeezing blood-filled leeches over his shirt front. But his ploys eventually worked and she agreed to marry him, despite it being completely unlawful; she was not an 'approved choice' and worse, she was a Catholic. The Prince, of course, when crowned king, would become Head of the Church of England.

The Prince of Wales, later King George IV, 'chained in love' to Maria Fitzherbert

So they secretly married, in the stately surroundings of... the front room of Mrs Fitzherbert's London home, in December 1785. The only clergyman the Prince could find to perform the ceremony - the Reverend John Burt - was locked up in London's Fleet prison, for being in debt. The Prince managed to get him out and paid him

£500 for performing the ceremony (Burt also said he had to be made a bishop when the Prince became king!). Just five people were present, two of them signing the marriage certificate, which the Prince had duly written out himself in his own, best handwriting!

Did the Prince tell his father, King George III, what he'd done? Of course not! And later, as rumours grew, the marriage was officially and categorically denied in Parliament – *several* times! Surprise, surprise!

The Prince and 'Mrs Prince' (as the locals called her) stayed in Brighton during the summer months, returning to London for the winter. As the marriage was secret (but everyone knew about it by now), they occupied different houses;

Portrait of Mrs Fitzherbert

he of course lodged in the Pavilion and she stayed in property close by. Later she lived in Old Steine, at Steine House, which still stands at the corner of Steine Lane. The Prince often appeared on the balcony here, with a broad grin on his face, but no one ever saw him depart from the Pavilion, leading to speculation there was a secret tunnel between his place and hers (a romantic notion, but highly unlikely).

But our George never could be loyal to any woman and had an affair with an actress named Anna Maria Crouch in the early 1790s. As the playwright Sheridan said, 'he was too much every lady's man to be the man of any lady.' He later returned to Maria and seemed happy and settled, but as the years slipped by, it was clear a proper, *legal* wife would have to be found for the young heir to the throne - and some offspring produced to succeed him too.

So, one Caroline of Brunswick (a German cousin) was accordingly produced, marrying the Prince in 1795, purely for political reasons and so he could get more money from Parliament to start paying off his vast debts (he had no idea of the value of money; in 1792 it's known he was £370,000 in debt – millions in today's money). The fickle Prince abruptly ended his relationship with Maria in 1794, by a simple, blunt letter, informing her it was all off. This wasn't just because he was about to officially marry - although he was - it was also because he was having another affair, this time with a Lady Jersey, a forty-year old grandmother!

Queen Caroline herself (oh dear, how to put this?) was a crude, unhygienic woman whom the Prince instantly hated. The day of his wedding, in April 1795, George was so drunk he had to be 'assisted' up the aisle and was so repulsed by his new bride he spent his honeymoon night drunk and burbling in a fireplace! She deserves some sympathy though as the Prince was generally pretty horrible to her whenever he could be. Once, he received a message stating, 'Your worst enemy is dead.' He's supposed to have coolly replied, 'Oh, is she?'

However, they consummated the marriage rapidly (the Prince openly admitted they only had sex three times) and a daughter – Princess Charlotte - was born, nine months after the wedding, in 1796. With the succession to the throne seemingly secure, George and Caroline immediately separated. When news of this got out, the outrage was so vociferous the Prince spent the 1796 season hiding at Bognor, rather than Brighton, to avoid the flak that was flying.

Caroline of Brunswick with Princess Charlotte

The *main* reason for the separation, other than the fact the Prince couldn't stand Caroline, was that his fervour for Mrs Fitzherbert had flared up again and he pleaded (oh, how he pleaded!) for a reunion. He altered his will leaving everything to her and even had the Pope state that Maria was his true wife in the eyes of God. He even tried the suicide stunt again. It took several years for her to capitulate, but eventually, in 1799, they were reconciled. He'd parted from Lady Jersey by now and we learn that for Maria, the years that followed 'were the happiest of her connection with the Prince.' She herself told Lord Stourton, that they were 'extremely poor, but as merry as crickets.'

Regrettably, fickle fellow that he was, George would have yet another affair, this time with a Lady Hertford, and finally separated from Maria in 1811 in a seemingly quite reasonable way. They met up occasionally, at various functions, he'd bow, she would curtsy, but that was about it.

Did they have children? There has been endless supposition about this over the years. Now proven beyond all doubt, by the brilliant research of Jim and Phillipa Foord-Kelcey, in their 1991 book, *Mrs Fitzherbert and Sons*, it's clear they had *seven* children. With the help of a small, trusted circle of friends, it was possible for them, masquerading as a family called Payne (Maria's maiden name), to live secretly among the English country gentry, with hardly anyone knowing their proper identity.

But then another quandary flared up in the early 1800s, of a totally different kind, which probably put affairs of the heart way down the Prince's list of priorities.

King George III, his father, had become unfit to rule and people thought he was going mad. He probably had porphyria, a metabolism problem, which can cause delirium. In 1811, a Parliamentary bill was passed, upping George's title to that of Prince Regent, making him monarch in all but title, despite the real king being alive and kicking. Power must have made George go a bit soft in the head too, for in 1820 he had Caroline put on trial for – of all things – adultery! Remember, all this is true. Parliament intervened and wisely withdrew the charge.

George, Prince Regent, was finally crowned King George IV in 1821 (he had Caroline locked out of the coronation ceremony) and he would rule for just ten years. But this epic love story must have its 'ahhh' ending - and it does!

George was sixty-seven when he died. The Duke of Wellington found a locket on his body, as it lay in the open coffin. It enclosed a miniature portrait of guess who? Yes, Maria – the real love of his life - and was duly buried with him. She had a matching one containing George's portrait, which she left in her will to Minnie, one of her daughters.

Mrs Fitzherbert, who must be one of the most long-suffering, forbearing and forgiving women ever seduced by royalty, died in Brighton, in 1837, aged eighty. She is buried in St John the Baptist's Church, Kemp Town, where her memorial has her wearing *three* wedding rings. And, incidentally, in 1833, after the death of George IV, Mrs Fitzherbert's key lawyer, Lord Stourton, asked her to sign a declaration he had written on the back of the marriage certificate testifying that her union with the late king was 'without issue' (in other words, no children). She refused.

Only Brighton could come up with an astonishing love story like this!

There's a postscript – or should that be post-mortem? - to the Prince's story. The examination into the causes of his death makes for appalling reading. We won't linger on it, except to say he died after 'passing a large evacuation mixed with blood.' He weighed over twenty stone, had a tumour the size of an orange on his bladder and his heart was 'grossly enlarged' and surrounded by a wall of solid fat.

His last words are said to have been, 'this is death.' It certainly was!

Let's move on!

Fire at the King's Chapel

Mrs Fitzherbert was a prolific letter writer and, on 14th December 1823, she wrote of a bizarre fire which took place in what she calls 'the King's Chapel', which stood in the Pavilion grounds at the Castle Square corner. It was removed after Queen Victoria sold the Pavilion off in 1850 (see page 26) and rebuilt in Montpelier Place where, at present, it serves as a day centre. By the time of the letter, George was King of England:

The Old King's Chapel

'*Everybody who could gain admission went to the King's Chapel this morning. The panel behind His Majesty took fire and the congregation were nearly suffocated. Sparks of fire made the appearance in the Chapel, but as His Majesty did not move, all the company sat quiet, frightened out of their wits, as none of them dared stir. After about three-quarters of an hour, when the fear of being burned had subsided, the windows were thrown open, and then people nearly died of the cold, but so far everyone has escaped unhurt.*'

Shooting at the Pavilion

One of the most amusing incidents to take place at the Royal Pavilion was on an evening when yet another grand ball was in progress and the Prince, probably a bit bored, went into a side room with some ladies and started showing off his skills with a small rifle. He shot at a target placed at the end of the room, then unwisely suggested the ladies have a try. One shot a hole in a door, another disfigured the ceiling, and when

The Prince entertaining at the Pavilion

Lady Downshire took her turn, she promptly discharged it through another door – which was open - shooting a violinist playing in the orchestra!

This is quite a well-known story and entirely true. It features in a letter written by a Mrs Creevey, to her husband in London, dated 29th October 1805. She was at the Pavilion when it happened!

More Shooting!

So was the Prince a good shot? Perhaps, perhaps not. In 1785, a press item, with a heading of *Le Roi s'amuse*, reads:

'On Monday, June 27, His Royal Highness mused himself on the Steyne for some time in attempting to shoot doves with single balls; but with what result we have not heard, though the Prince is esteemed a most excellent shot, and seldom presents his piece without doing some execution. The Prince, in the course of his diversion, either by design or accident, lowered the tops of several of the chimneys of the Hon. Mr. Windam's house.'

King George III

George III

King George III, at a time when he was calm and didn't appear to be going insane, was induced by his son to visit Brighton. After a hasty look round, he declared, 'Treeless land, shadeless shore, shipless sea.' And promptly returned to London!

The Barrys

More outrageous capers with George IV! When he was Prince of Wales, he kept some thoroughly dreadful company when staying at Brighton, particularly with a trio of youths from an aristocratic family named Barrymore. These young 'bucks' (they had a sister too, who swore, it's said, like a fish seller) were of Irish descent, incredibly rich and thoroughly decadent. Even as boys – 'left without parents from an early age,' we are told - they were up to no good, at one time going out at the dead of night with carpenters' tools and changing all the inn signs around in the area where they lived. The eldest, Richard, nick-named 'Hellgate', had been a mere four years old when he inherited the Irish earldom of Barrymore, which included two massive estates (one in Ireland, another in England), plus an annual income of over £10,000 a year.

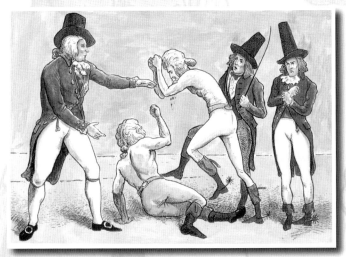

The Barry Brothers - Richard has the nose-bleed!

The two oldest brothers, Richard (just twenty years old) and Henry, arrived in Brighton in 1788. The third brother, in France at this time, would join them later. They wasted no time in getting up to all sorts of mischief and taking part in silly contests, betting huge sums of money they could complete any challenge set them. Every wager to do with horses was instantly taken up as Richard was a skilled horseman and could often be found racing other coaches around the Steine in a cloud of dust. The Prince of Wales frequently kept their company (he liked all this messing about too) and once came scurrying out of the Pavilion to act as referee in a fight Richard had picked with a man named Fox, whose father, so he thought, had insulted him in a newspaper article.

But it was the Prince himself who got the shock of his life one night at the Pavilion when he woke to find a donkey in his bedroom, with a large pair of horns fixed to its head and fireworks attached to its body – somehow smuggled in, of course, by the Barrys.

People sometimes got the better of them though, such as when Richard was challenged by a man named Bullock to a running race. This seemed no contest, as

Bullock was huge, weighed some eighteen stone and could be beaten even if they walked it. But Bullock stipulated, as part of the wager, that he could choose the course and be allowed a ten-yard start. Barrymore readily agreed and the Prince came over from the Pavilion to watch. Bullock craftily chose one of the narrowest lanes in the town for the race, supposedly Black Lion Lane (this still exists, of course), and being hemmed in by walls all the way along, Barrymore just couldn't get past him, so lost!

Another time saw Henry Barrymore (nick-named 'Cripplegate', because he had a club foot) challenged to a duel on the Steine, following an argument over a card game, which he duly accepted. His opponent was a stout and elderly Member of Parliament named Howarth. They met at five in the morning, the usual time for such activities it seems, and on taking their places, pistols ready, Howarth calmly began removing his clothes, until he stood facing his opponent in just his drawers. He said he'd been a doctor once and had learnt the importance of keeping wounds clean! Some shots were fired but the incident seems to have ended good-humouredly.

The most outrageous wager was when the Duke of Bedford offered Richard a thousand guineas (millions today!) if he would eat a cat alive, in front him – all of it. Declining himself, he went out and tried to induce some person or other to do it for him, even offering huge payment, but without success. So another bet was lost.

Black Lion Lane

Even Mrs Fitzherbert, the illegal wife of the Prince, wasn't spared a jolly jape or two. Henry was bet he couldn't ride a horse all the way up the stairs of her house in the Steine. This was duly attempted, but having reached the top floor the animal refused to descend, so blacksmiths were sent for, to 'persuade' it down. Mrs Fitzherbert, we learn, was very amused by the whole incident.

The Barrys delighted too in shocking residents and visitors with outrageous jokes and behaviour, which they thought terribly funny. One bit of fun was to prop an open coffin, complete with dummy corpse, up against someone's front door (at night), ring the bell, then hide to enjoy what followed.

Whoever opened the door would have the corpse slump down into their house causing, no doubt, screams of consternation from any ladies and probably causing one or two to faint (which was the idea). They did this at other times with a servant playing the corpse, suitably dressed and covered with white powder, who would step out of the coffin and stagger into the house scaring everyone witless. On one occasion the servant was shot at!

All this buffoonery clearly affected the general staidness of the town; we learn that the use of the stocks (the frame that held sitting prisoners by their two ankles) was so stretched for drunken behaviour that often, 'there being but four holes, one leg alone of each delinquent was secured.'

It comes as no surprise to learn that Richard Barrymore was killed at the age of just twenty-four, when a gun at his side unintentionally discharged, shooting him straight through the eye. Henry inherited the family title only to find his departed brother had squandered some £300,000 in just three years (again, equal to millions today) and there was only £5,000 left to the family fortune. The youngest brother, Augustus – known as 'Newgate', supposedly the only prison he hadn't been in - decided to take holy orders! Perhaps this is why there are no further stories of crazy capers in Brighton and we are told that 'the name of Barry, a family whose follies had enlivened England, lingered only as a memory...'

It's hard to believe all this clowning around went on in Brighton some two hundred years ago, perpetrated by the very top aristocratic inhabitants of the town. And we wonder at the behaviour of *today's* youth!

A Regency Blood

When we think of the 'bucks' and 'rakes' of Brighton – such as the Barrys - we tend to visualise immaculately-dressed but irresponsible young men, with a 'don't give a damn' attitude to life. As we've just seen, mischief-making, drinking and gambling were their main pastimes, with a good deal of flirting and womanising also high on the priority list.

The Barrys apart, is this image true though? Judging from the following amazing piece of self-declaration, published in *The Sporting Magazine* of November 1800, it's entirely accurate!

'Rose at nine - rumpled my wig, and stood before the glass an hour endeavouring to give myself a sloven-like appearance. Having at length succeeded in making myself a complete blackguard, walked to the bathing place – Lady Dashaway told me I had been up all night – smiled assent. Memorandum, always affect the Rake, its stylish, and the women like it. Took my position on the cliffs so as to prevent the ladies bathing – Damned good fun! Though the other morning got my nose pulled

by a crusty old Gentleman, merely for asking to bathe in the machine with his daughter. Dull dog. Not one of us could take such a joke, so passed it over, though a shameful report was circulated at the Libraries that I declined, because the old man was a notorious fighting character. All a hum! Can hit a card at ten paces when my nerves are steady, and ain't frightened.

At twelve o'clock, knowing the libraries and the Steine crowded, went with a party of spirited witty Dogs and bathed in view of the Ladies, though a damned unlucky accident happened, for a party of Wags, having seized our clothes, bribed the old bathing lady to follow us into the water. We made for shore, could not find our clothes. What the devil was to be done? Boys pelted us, Women hissed us. Dogs barked, children shouted, men swore.

At last, hearing a sour fellow talk of the pillory, made a precipitate retreat, and, covered with mud, rotten eggs and other sweet-scented accompaniments, arrived at home, departed quick for London, and left my bills unpaid, and my character behind me!'

A typical Regency 'buck'

William IV and Queen Victoria

William IV

William IV, who succeeded George IV (they were brothers), stayed at the Pavilion at least once every year of his reign (1830-37). Servants and friends thought he was practically teetotal compared with George IV, as he only drunk a pint of sherry with his dinner. He was also wonderfully idiosyncratic; once, at a New Year's Eve ball, his dancing partner was a sixty-one year old admiral! He didn't share his brother's interest in architecture or the decorative arts, saying all that sort of thing was just

Queen Victoria

'knick-knackery.' William had ten children, all by an actress named Dora Jordan (did she have any time for acting?!), but none by his wife, so when he died, in 1837, it was his niece who became Queen - Queen Victoria. She also used the Royal Pavilion as a seaside residence, but found the early railway trippers irksome, and gave up the Pavilion for the amity of Osborne House on the Isle of Wight.

But she removed all the furniture and fittings from the Pavilion – even the wallpaper was carefully peeled off - and 143 vans took the contents away in 1847-48. The Commissioners of Brighton, forerunner of the Council, bought it from her in 1850 more or less as an empty shell.

John Butcher and his Fly

The term 'fly by night', still given in most dictionaries as meaning an irresponsible person, has its origins in the small Brighton vehicle seen in this 1820's print of King's Road, the main thoroughfare that runs along the seafront. It's part of the view we saw earlier of Sake Deen Mahomed's shampooing premises. The 'fly' was the invention of local carpenter, John Butcher, then living in Jew Street, who became a cripple in 1809, following a fall while employed building the Royal Stables (now the Dome concert hall). He soon devised a small covered invalid carriage on wheels

John Butcher's 'fly' (see wider version, p14)

for his family and friends to push him around the town. More were built for commercial use (replacing the old sedan chair arrangement, which had no wheels) and soon a small fleet were operating in Brighton, a kind of early taxi service, with fares charged – and it's true - according to the size of customer.

The Prince and his young 'buck' friends - such as the Barrys - were frequent patrons and their womanising escapades led to the

Prince himself christening them 'flys' possibly because they were small, fast little carriages buzzing here, there and everywhere, resembling their insect counterparts, or because they were often employed for getting away from some nocturnal indulgence extremely quickly. Either way, the name stuck and the subsequent term 'fly by night' entered the English language - still in use two hundred years later.

Harriet Mellon

This woman had her eye firmly on the older, wealthy man. And when we say wealthy, we don't mean just comfortably off, as you'll see.

Born in November 1777, at Lambeth, London, the illegitimate daughter of a wardrobe mistress from a 'strolling players' type of theatre company, she became a successful actress herself, even appearing at Drury Lane, London. She also performed once at Brighton's Duke Street theatre, where the transvestite Chevalier d'Eon fenced (page 9). Why this woman is particularly interesting is because in 1815 she married eighty-three year old Thomas Coutts, head of Coutts and Company, the royal bank of the day (he was a mere 42 years older than her) after being his mistress for a number of years. On his death, in 1822, aged ninety-one, she inherited a huge estate and other property; in round terms something like £1,800,000. She also inherited a nick-name – 'Mrs Millions'.

Thomas Coutts

Harriet Mellon

The Brighton connection is that among several properties she acquired was 131 King's Road, on the corner of Regency Square. As a widow she became a senior partner in the Coutts bank, lending money to royalty (even George IV!). She next married the twenty-six year-old William Beauclerk, the 9th Duke of St Albans (twenty-three years younger than her) in June 1827, a direct descendant of Charles II, who was Hereditary Grand Falconer of England. He held hawking parties on the Downs and sometimes displayed his birds in Regency Square. The

The house at the corner of Regency Square

marriage was childless and Harriet Mellon died in August 1837, one of the richest women in Britain. The family fortune, by the way, went to Coutts' granddaughter. She spent huge amounts on a wide range of charitable causes and funded several notable buildings such as St Stephen's Church, Westminster and the Columbia Market in northeast London. She also provided the ornate drinking fountain at the Zoological Gardens, Regent's Park.

Sir Walter Scott

The famous author of *Ivanhoe* and *Rob Roy* gets a quick mention in passing because of a bizarre declaration he made once about the ancient hill fort at Devil's Dyke. There are twenty-five ancient hill forts in Sussex; the wooden palisades that enclosed them

have long since gone and all that's left are the circular earthen banks and ditches that once surrounded the fort interior. They were basically homesteads and meeting places for trading and retreating, if need be, against raids from other tribes. The one at Devil's Dyke dates from the late Iron Age and now it's quite hard to make out exactly where it is – a few high banks can be climbed, a hundred or so yards from the pub, but not much more.

However, on a visit in 1828, Scott declared the fort must have been, 'a rampart of great strength and depth, enclosing, I presume, the precincts of a British town that must have held 30,000 men at least.' He was at a loss, though, to discover where they obtained their water.

Sir Walter Scott

The *town* of Devil's Dyke? There's a thought!

Harriet Howard

Now for *the* most amazing 'rags to riches' story involving a Brighton woman. From vermin to ermine, one might say!

The story starts in a slum area of Brighton between North Street and Church Street and a mean courtyard named Gerards Court. This dated from the early 1800s and was swept away in 1936, when much of the town's substandard housing was demolished. The site today is hard to determine, but a few old walls near the car park in King Place may be part of it. An alleyway, leading to the site, lasted until the 1970s.

Here, in August 1823, to a bookmaking father, was born Elizabeth Ann Haryett, whose grandfather was owner of the Castle Inn (where Castle Square gets its name from). When she was fifteen she ran off to London to live with a well-known jockey, Jem Mason. She became an aspiring actress and took the name Harriet Howard. At eighteen she was involved with the already-married Major Mountjoy Martyn of the Life Guards, and bore him a son, who at the baptism was made out to be the child of her

Gerards Court in the 1930s

parents. The grateful Major Martyn, spared a scandal, bestowed a small fortune on her (and the child).

Then it gets *very* interesting! At a party in London, sometime in 1846, Miss Howard met the exiled Prince Louis Philippe Napoleon, nephew of the famous Napoleon Bonaparte, who had his eyes firmly fixed on the throne of France his uncle once occupied. He'd been exiled (and imprisoned, but he escaped) because the French government knew he might make a political move sometime or other and that if he achieved any kind of power he would be as disastrous for France as his notorious uncle had been.

Louis Philippe became infatuated with Miss H and moved in with her. During the following months, using that small fortune from Major Martyn, she supported his efforts - and several conspiracies - to return him to France, which duly happened (it's a long story!) and he was elected President of the French Republic in 1848. It

Harriet Howard

was Miss Howard again who largely financed the necessary 1851 coup d'état, which enabled him to establish an imperial government the following year. In 1853, he was finally crowned Napoleon III, Emperor of the French. However, searching for an empress, he cast Miss Howard aside, settling for a stunningly beautiful woman, Eugenie de Montijo, 'who had shoulders, when shoulders mattered.' Howard retreated to Le Havre when the marriage was announced... and waited.

Miss Howard's fortune gradually built up again as Napoleon dutifully repaid his financial

Napoleon III

obligations to her. She was given the title Comtesse de Beauregard and installed in a chateau near Paris.

Within six months of the marriage, the wait was over and Napoleon resumed his relationship with her, but his wife (who apparently found sex 'disgusting'), discovered what was going on, and naturally enough put her small foot down. He, being in need of a legal heir and some sort of respectability, had to acquiesce.

Eventually in 1854, Miss Howard distanced herself from Napoleon and married a Captain Clarence Trelawny, an English horse breeder who cheerfully used her money to further his business interests. However, the marriage didn't last – she obviously wasn't used to such a settled situation – and they divorced in 1865. The same year, in November, she died. And it's hard to follow that story!

Only we can...

Lady Abinger

Here's another lady with an amazing story – and amazing energy! Sex, murder, infatuation, incarceration – it's hard to beat Lady Abinger's outrageous tale...

Her story involves the house seen here through the arches of the 'Birdcage Bandstand' on the seafront just after World War II. This was Abinger House, the last private mansion to survive on King's Road. There was an earlier property on the site called Westcliff House, but this was rebuilt in the 1850s and later became Abinger House when occupied for many years by a Lord and Lady Abinger. He was a titled aristocrat, but in respectable, earlier days, Lady Abinger was Marguerite Steinheil, an extremely rampant lady and a prominent member of

Abinger House

French society. Her name was linked to all sorts of composers and artists in the 1880s and 1890s, plus any number of politicians; she's also believed to have been the occasional playmate of Russia's Grand Duke Vladimir and even had a fling or two with the King of Siam.

Marguerite Steinheil

But she achieved lasting notoriety when involved with the French President Felix Faure, who'd come to office in 1895. The official explanation for her daily visits was to help write his memoirs, a task that often went on very late into the night. Unfortunately, it was during one of these urgent sessions at the Paris Elysee, in February 1899 that the President, aged fifty-eight, having taking some 'stimulatory pills' (early Viagra?), suffered apoplexy (a cerebral haemorrhage) and died. When aides hurried in, Miss Steinheil was found to be completely naked. To be discovered with one corpse in life is bad enough, particularly in the nude, but nine years later she was discovered with two more. One was her artist husband – Alphonse Steinheil - the other, her elderly mother, both strangled. She herself was found gagged and tied to her bed. Her state of dress on this occasion went unrecorded. The explanation of what had happened - according to her - was that four mysterious hooded figures broke into her house and proceeded to murder her husband and her mother. At first, suspicious though it all was, no charges were brought against her, but

Felix Faure

later, caught trying to plant evidence that would shift suspicion onto a servant, she was arrested and incarcerated in the vile Saint-Lazare prison.

Her subsequent trial caused a worldwide media sensation. Despite giving conflicting evidence, she put on a virtuoso 'helpless little woman' performance and, to a mixture of cheers and gasps, the all-male jury, whom she'd completed bewitched, declared her innocent. A barrister who'd been present at the trial – Robert Scarlett, later to become the 6th Lord Abinger – took a fancy to her and proposed. She refused him at first, but they were later married in 1917. So she became Lady Abinger and the house on Brighton's seafront became their seaside residence. He died ten years later and she moved from Abinger House to 24 Adelaide Crescent, where she wrote her memoirs. Yet despite her extraordinary life, she died,

The Abinger Coach

unnoticed, in a Hove nursing home in 1954. In the meantime, the seafront house had been occupied by Lord Wakehurst - MP for Brighton from 1889-1905 - who died in 1936. The house saw military use during World War II and was eventually demolished in 1948. A Regency-style pub – going under the name of The Abinger - occupied the site, which in turn was replaced by the Kingsley Court block of flats, presently on the site, in 1987. Brighton Museum had Lord and Lady Abinger's coach on show for many years in its main ground floor gallery (now the principal art and furniture display). There's also an Abinger Road in Portslade.

Charles Dickens

Charles Dickens

One of the weirdest incidents to take place in West Street, in the Old Town area, occurred when Charles Dickens, the famous author, was staying at no. 60 early in 1849. He was a frequent visitor to Brighton between 1837 and 1868, but while staying at West Street, the landlord of his lodgings quite suddenly went totally berserk for some unaccountable reason and ran completely amok. His daughter went mad too at exactly the same time. Understandably, Dickens fled and booked in at the Bedford Hotel on the seafront. Unfortunately, why 'mine host' and his daughter went instantaneously crazy isn't recorded, nor what happened to them subsequently.

Azimoolah Khan and the Indian Mutiny

Now for the Devil's Dyke Hotel and its supposed link with the notorious Indian Mutiny of 1857.

The Indian Mutiny was the bloodiest rebellion in the history of the British Empire. It began with a large-scale uprising by native soldiers (known as sepoys) against their colonial masters, and developed into general rebellion as thousands of civilians joined in. It took over a year to quell and thousands – on both sides – were killed. It led to India being taken over completely by the British government and Queen Victoria crowned Queen Empress of the sub-continent.

There were many reasons why tensions erupted into widespread rebellion, but essentially it was felt the British presence was eroding Indian traditions and riding roughshod over its religion and heritage.

Matters came to a head when a certain type of rifle was issued to Indian troops. The rumour spread that its cartridges were greased with pig and cow fat, thus offending both Moslems and Hindus. In February 1857 the 19th Bengal Native Infantry refused to use the cartridges, leading to the troop being disbanded.

But the mutiny began in earnest at Meerut in May 1857 when over eighty members of the 3rd Bengal Light Cavalry were imprisoned for refusing the cartridges and were rescued by Indian comrades. The following day Delhi was attacked and fell to the mutineers. News of these events spread rapidly, leading to further mutinies elsewhere. Eventually all Bengal cavalry regiments and most of the infantry regiments were affected. Some were disarmed before they had the chance to mutiny while in other cases British officers refused to doubt the loyalty of their men until it was too late.

Many local rulers supported the mutineers, having been disturbed by Britain's seizure of native states. There were only 35,000 British soldiers in the whole sub-continent and these were widely scattered. Furthermore, reinforcements took months to arrive. Fortunately for the British the mutiny was almost exclusively confined to the Bengal Army. The Madras and Bombay armies were relatively unaffected and other units, including Sikhs, Punjabi Moslems and Gurkhas, remained loyal. But it all got pretty nasty, as you'll see.

But what's this revolt in far off India got to do with the Devil's Dyke Hotel? It's because in 1854 one Nana Sahib (who was the adopted son of a chief minister of the Maratha people of central India) sent a high ranking representative - Azimoolah Khan - to Britain, to persuade the

A scene from the Indian Mutiny

The Nana Sahib

East India Company (a London-based business group that dominated India's financial affairs at this time) to continue paying him a pension granted to his father when he was alive. This they refused, on the grounds that he was adopted, not a blood relative. While in Britain, Khan dressed in western clothes and met up with Dickens, Carlyle, Macaulay, Tennyson and Thackeray, and also saw Queen Victoria, whom he described as 'a squat little woman in the sway of her German husband.' However, Azimoolah Khan was not particularly well during his visit and on doctor's advice, spent some time in Sussex at the Devil's Dyke Hotel (given, no doubt, the old 'purity of the local air will do you good' recommendation). While in residence, he sent many, many dispatches to his miffed master, so totally disproportionate to the business of the pension that it's thought he was acting as a spy and relaying 'intelligence' on British affairs.

The Nana Sahib subsequently took a leading part in the Indian Mutiny and was guilty of the infamous Massacre of Cawnpore, near the River Ganges, where most of the men defending the place were shot, and two hundred British women and children subsequently butchered to death in a bloodbath. It's even thought that the first draft of the proclamation inciting the Indians to rise up in mutiny was drawn up by Azimoolah Khan while staying at the hotel, but that's probably taking the story a bit too far! Although... having said that, the proclamation was printed on a press that Khan picked up somewhere on his trip to and from India!

Dinapore Street (left) in the early 1960s

Incidentally, there used to be a Dinapore Street in Brighton, running between Richmond Street and Albion Hill. This was built in 1859-60 and obviously named after Dinapore in India, a place connected with the Indian Mutiny. It had three pubs; The Live and Let Live on its Richmond Street Corner, the Obed Arms at the Albion Hill end (Obed being another Indian location), and the other pub was The Gun Tavern (also possibly linked with the mutiny), a few doors along from the Obed Arms. The street was demolished late in 1965.

Martin Leonard Landfried

Staying with things military, during the Charge of the Light Brigade of October 1854, the disastrous blunder where 673 mounted troops charged straight at a battery of blazing Russian cannons (*The Times* called it 'an atrocity without parallel'), the bugler who sounded the fateful charge came from Lewes. He was Martin Leonard Landfried, who joined the army in 1849, when he was barely fifteen

The Charge of the Light Brigade

years old. He survived the Charge – he was wounded and his horse shot dead under him - and later joined the 1st Sussex Royal Garrison Artillery (volunteers) in 1865, becoming their bandmaster in 1890. And in what seems a very early example of 'related merchandising', a gramophone record was issued that year of him playing the famous charge (using the original bugle), accompanied by a spoken introduction. One or two or these records are still around today.

Reunion picture of the Charge survivors

In the late 1890s, a reunion of Light Brigade survivors was arranged as a newspaper stunt. Among several Sussex veterans, of whom Landfried was one, two others were found living in Brighton. Landfried's grave is in the cemetery south of Old Shoreham Road, Hove. Why he's not buried in his native town of Lewes doesn't seem to be known.

And just for the record (pun unintended), the last survivor of the Charge was Trooper James Hewitt who died aged ninety-five in July 1926. He's in the photo somewhere!

Landfried's grave in Hove cemetery

Henry Holden

Even with 'Custer's Last Stand', as the Battle of the Little Big Horn has become known, there's a Brighton connection. The encounter took place in June 1876 near the Little Big Horn River in Montana where nearly six hundred men of the 7th Cavalry Regiment, led by Custer - plus about fifty scouts and civilians - fought a pitched battle against hordes of Lakota Sioux and Cheyenne Indians.

Among them was Henry Holden, born in Brighton (one source says London), who'd joined the US army at Boston and subsequently Custer's troops in 1872. He risked his life by fetching ammunition from a packhorse while his division was pinned down by hordes of circling Indians.

Holden survived the conflict – unlike Custer and most of his other men – and was awarded the Congressional Medal of Honour for bravery. On retirement, he came to England and lived in Whitehawk Road then Rugby Place, Brighton, where he died in December 1905, aged sixty-nine. He's buried in Brighton's Bear Road cemetery and his medal is on permanent display at the Valley Forge National Park, Pennsylvania.

Holden's grave

Vincent van Gogh

Down the years, all manner of famous people have visited Brighton for one reason or another. In a letter of March 1876 to his brother Theo, a young Vincent van Gogh, then staying at Ramsgate, Kent, mentions the pleasure he'd had walking to Brighton while staying in London three years earlier, probably when at 87 Hackford Road, Brixton (he'd stayed somewhere else in London a bit earlier, but the address isn't known). He was working in the shop of Goupil & Cie, a firm of international art dealers, in Southampton Street, just off the Strand. His salary was £90 a year.

Van Gogh was trying his hand at drawing at this time, but it wouldn't be until 1879 that he started painting seriously. He was a formidable walker though and we can only guess what he saw and – possibly – sketched, as he made his way, presumably, down the London Road, to the Steine and the sea. And what on earth did his young artist's eye make of the Royal Pavilion?

Vincent van Gogh
as a young man

Gypsy Lee

This was a Brighton fortune teller who worked from a caravan at the Devil's Dyke. Early in the summer of 1902, she foretold that the coronation of Edward VII (Queen Victoria's eldest son) would not take place. This shocked everyone as all the arrangements had been made for what would be a huge national and international event and the date clearly fixed for 9th June 1902.

Edward VII

Why wouldn't the King be crowned? Was some terrible disaster about to strike? Only the fortune teller wasn't surprised when news came that the coronation was postponed - the King had developed acute appendicitis!

Gypsy Lee outside her Dyke caravan

Edward was crowned one month later, on 9th August. Gypsy Lee's further fame was assured of course, and no doubt the queues outside her caravan were especially long that season.

Gypsy Lee actually lived in Melbourne Street, taking a carriage to the Dyke each day, where she worked for nearly forty years. In 1904, she was fined for trading illegally. She then ran refreshment rooms for a while, but eventually languished at an asylum in Haywards Heath, where she died in 1911.

James Doughty

July 1911 saw the marriage of James Doughty to Alice Zilpah Underwood, at Brighton's Registry Office. He was ninety-two, she was twenty-five. Read that last sentence again! Both are seen in the photograph here, where Doughty, an ex-circus performer, is working a dog act on the West Pier. He'd been an entertainer for nearly eighty years, having run away from home, in Bristol, to join a circus. He formed his act, 'Doughty's Dogs', and toured it very successfully, even performing in front of Queen Victoria at one time. But he ended up on the pier and, presumably, that is where he met his new bride to be (his previous wife had only been dead four months!)

James Doughty and his dogs on the West Pier, about 1910 - Alice Zilpah Underwood is on the left

'I've been very lonely,' he told the press. She's a good woman. We're both children of God.'

On the wedding day, so many people turned up at his home – 19 Middle Street – that the police had to intervene and clear a way through for the carriage, which would take them to the ceremony at Prince's Street. The bridegroom was wearing a multi-coloured suit, a gaudy tie and bright cap and he cracked jokes all the way there. His bride, from Montpelier Road, was described in the *Brighton Gazette* as being a, 'slim, good-looking young woman very neatly dressed in blue and white voile, wearing a large straw hat trimmed with forget-me-knots.'

At the ceremony, there were a few raised eyebrows when Doughty produced the ring – a gaudy, 'over the top' theatrical one, of huge size and weight. Then, with a wink, he produced the real one, but put it first, 'by accident' on the bridesmaid's finger.

Congratulations came from all over the country; wedding presents included a five pound note from the flamboyant art collector Alfred Rothschild.

19 Middle Street – where James Doughty lived

Doughty was obviously on a real high as the crowds showered him and Alice with confetti. 'I want to live to be a hundred,' he declared. 'Then I shall put on my old clown's dress and show you what a clown was like in the old days.'

Sadly, Doughty died two years after the wedding from pneumonia, leaving very little to his young wife. She said she hadn't married him for money anyway, but 'to care for him in his old age.'

Hippodrome Deaths

Just before – and just after – World War I, the Grim Reaper must have been sitting in the stalls of Brighton's famous Hippodrome Theatre of Varieties in Middle Street, as a number of fatal incidents occurred.

Auguste van Biene appeared in January 1913, with a sketch called *The Broken Melody*, which finished with him playing the tune of that name on his cello. He'd performed this act some 6000 times in theatres across the world and the 'melody' was published as sheet music for the public to buy. While on stage at the Hippodrome, with a packed house before him, playing his cello, he dropped dead. Was there a doctor in the house? Actually there was, but too late.

Harry Fragson was a popular Anglo-French comedian, who'd had a huge success with the song, *Hullo, Hullo, Who's Your Lady Friend?* After appearing at the Hippodrome in December 1913, he went to France to visit his much deranged father, who was staying at a hotel in Paris. When Fragson appeared, his father produced a gun and instantly shot him dead.

Harry Fragson

Sheet music cover showing Auguste van Biene at his cello

In July 1922, Marie Lloyd appeared at the Hippodrome, but was clearly unwell and again, the Grim Reaper was smiling. Someone who saw her at this time wrote; 'I received a shock, for, I beheld, not the Marie I had known, but a

Marie Lloyd

shadow, a wreck of a woman who had charmed my youthful heart in three Drury Lane pantomimes and on the halls. 'I'm One of the Ruins that Cromwell Knocked About a Bit' she sang or rather croaked. It was, to everyone present, a painful sight to watch the feeble attempts of a slowly dying woman to repeat her past triumphs. Night after night, throughout the week, poor Marie, tottering, helpless, and conscious of her infirmity, had to be literally carried to her dressing room. It was the beginning of the end.'

Marie Lloyd died the following October at just fifty-two years old.

George Smythe and Magician Ling Look

And while on theatrical matters, let's jump back to the 1880s and an appalling story about a fatality in another Brighton playhouse.

It happened at the Oxford Theatre of Varieties in New Road. This was just a few doors along from the Theatre Royal; it surprises everyone to learn two theatres existed in New Road, almost alongside each other, but they did. The Oxford is seen here (opposite) in the early 1900s, when it was called the Court, but it looked exactly the same at the time of this story.

On 27th December 1881, a young lad named George Smythe (from nearby Foundry Street) and a friend - Henry Stockley - tried to get in to see the Theatre Royal's pantomime, *Dick Whittington*, but found it sold out, so walked a few doors down to see what was on at the Oxford. It was a variety bill, including Monsieur Zampi, the only one-legged gymnast in the world, comic impersonations from Mr Wilfred Roxby, the Brothers Morton in a minstrel act, plus illusionist Ling Look, 'the Great Chinese Salamander, Lord of Fire, Cannon and Sword'. In they went!

The lads jostled along the front row of the gallery and settled themselves for the 7.30 start. The show was hosted by traditional music hall Chairman, who introduced each act from his seat, on one side of the stage, and probably extolling the virtues of each act far more than they merited!

The show progressed until it was time for Ling Look, whose act consisted of several hair-raising stunts including swallowing a large number of eggs, applying a red-hot poker to his arm and drinking boiling oil. He also pushed a walking stick all the way down his throat, then a sword!

The climax of the act was - bizarrely - Look firing a cannon straight out into the audience. This looked heavy and formidable, but was actually made of lightweight wood, but had a metal lining inside which contained a simple wad of newspaper to keep the gunpowder in place. But for all the audience knew, it could have been a mass of shot he was about to shoot out at them. It was a stunt meant to scare and thrill the audience and to provide Look with his 'big finish'.

The preparations were made and the Chairman and Look urged everyone to crouch down. The cannon was set on two stands near the back of the stage. Look swallowed a sword, leaving the handle sticking upwards. He positioned himself under the cannon and lifted it on the sword hilt, perfectly balanced, and stood fully upright. Look's wife approached with a red hot poker – one he'd used earlier – to set it off. Look approached the front of the stage, then sank on one knee.

George's friend, Henry, was bending down with just his eyes above the rail. George was on his feet, craning forward, to get a better look.

There was a crash of music from the orchestra, the cannon exploded, but by a million to one chance, a piece of compacted newspaper, weighing only five-eighths of an ounce, hit George Smythe on the forehead instantly shattering his skull to smithereens. Bits of bone, blood and brains went everywhere and George's body slumped backwards, virtually headless. Chaos! Screaming people scrambled out of their seats, trying to get out of the gallery, the commotion quickly spreading down to the main body of the theatre. When a doctor eventually reached George's dead body, he found the rock-hard pellet of paper that had caused the fatality on the floor almost next to him.

The Court Theatre, about 1910, previously the Oxford Theatre of Varieties

Police arrived and Look and his wife were arrested and both charged with murder. The inquest on the body was speedily held the very next day.

Look's trial was at the Lewes Assizes on 11th January 1882 – again very quickly after the event - but after a lengthy description of what actually happened, plus it being repeatedly stated that Look had done the same stunt many, many times, without injury to anyone - it only took the jury a matter of minutes to realise it was a 'one-off' incident and Look was found innocent.

George Smythe's funeral was attended by a thousand people, including Look's wife.

It was reported that 'so deeply affected was she that she would have fallen into the grave had she not been supported away.'

But we can only wonder what was said when members of the audience got home after the accident at the theatre. 'How was the show then?' 'Oh, it had to be stopped. Someone got their head blown off'.

Aleister Crowley

The next – literally - fantastic individual, takes us into the world of the occult and things get decidedly serious.

A 1960's view inside the theatre – it was demolished in 1963

On a December morning in 1947, a group of twenty-six, well-dressed men and women attended a funeral in the chapel of Woodvale Brighton Crematorium, off Lewes Road. All was silent and seemed normal, even though no priest was there to lead the service. But directly the coffin was brought in the congregation rose to their feet and began chanting black magic incantations, to the astonishment of the attendants and undertakers. 'Praise the great god Pan!' they chanted. 'We worship thee Satan!'

This was the funeral service of the world-famous and notorious black magician, Aleister Crowley, undoubtedly the most extraordinary person ever associated with Brighton.

His 'disciples' had travelled from all over Britain to attend the last rites of the most famous magician of modern times. Yet he was an amazingly talented man, being

Woodvale Chapel and crematorium

an expert chess player, a skilled mountain climber, a great traveller, a poet, and both a gifted writer and painter. But he was also a devil-worshipper, a pornographer and a charlatan, and indulged in such wanton acts of depravity that in the 1920s the popular press called him, 'the wickedest man in the world' – and the name stuck. In fact, he was credited with every vice and excess imaginable, including cannibalism, sex with animals, plus possessing the extremely disturbing ability to summon demons to do his bidding.

He was born in Warwickshire in 1875 and his father - a wealthy brewer and devout member of the Plymouth Brethern movement – brought him up extremely strictly, with regular Bible-reading sessions as part of a robust spiritual education. But Crowley rebelled, preferring to study the book's evil characters instead. His mother told him he would grow up like the Great Beast 666 of Revelations, a role he would willingly accept in later life.

In 1895, he attended Cambridge University. When his father died and a trust set up for him matured, Crowley left and started calling himself Brother Perdurabo (Latin for 'I will endure') and taking drugs. In 1904 came his *Book of the Law*, in which he claimed his mission was to destroy Christianity. He was, he claimed, the true messiah of the new age.

Three years later, he formed a magical society, 'The Order of the Silver Star' and also headed a German group which specialised in practising all sorts of erotic rites. Sex and magic were now to become his two main interests.

Like other self-styled messiahs, he invented extravagant titles and in turn called himself Prince Chioa Khan, Count Vladimar Svaroff, the Great Beast and even the demon Baphomet – usually depicted as half-man, half-goat - said by some to have been worshipped by the Knights Templars.

During World War I, he went to America and for some reason known best to him, wrote a stream of anti-British propaganda. Obviously, Christians regarded his activities with horror and he was soundly condemned in church sermons.

Aleister Crowley

His faithful followers were usually neurotic, weak, unhappy, lonely and sometimes ignorant people. It was mostly men who fell under his spell and they gave him the money to spend on drugs, drink, women and travelling.

One disciple – and lover - was the poet and author Victor Neuburg, who would later form a 'simple life' community near Storrington in Sussex. Neuburg, incidentally, is often credited with 'discovering' the young poet Dylan Thomas, when editing the poetry section of a journal known as the *Sunday Referee*. Together, Crowley and Neuberg travelled to Algeria and the Sahara Desert to perform an Enochian ritual, which would summon up a demon known as Chorizon. This would, Crowley believed, open up the gates of hell to him. Both became violently possessed during the ceremony, Crowley raving and behaving like a wild animal, with Neuburg struggling around on the ground with Chorizon, supposedly, trying to throttle him, before being subdued back in his dark abode. Neuburg fell ill after the encounter, but Crowley's powers – he claimed - increased tenfold, He said his influence over Neuburg was all for his good as both a writer and as a man, but in fact it was the ruination of him, and he became a drug addict, leading a very despondent life.

In 1920, Crowley went to Sicily with one of his many women lovers, who he called 'The Scarlet Woman' or 'Ape of Toth'. Three years later the Italian government, shocked by his behaviour and the strange people he attracted, deported him and a dozen of his followers.

And so it all went on. Crowley was constantly in the news for one shocking incident after another. But after wandering, often near-destitute, from country to country for a number of years, he returned to more or less permanent residence in England in 1929. He continued to attract followers to his magic and what he was then calling the 'Law of Thelema,' and it was they who helped finance the lavish books of poetry and magic writing he produced at this time. During World War II, he moved to a boarding house in Hastings, and he died there late in 1947, aged seventy-two.

After the bizarre funeral service at Woodvale, two Brighton Councillors called it 'a desecration of concentrated ground' and asked for an inquiry to ensure that in future only orthodox funerals could take place in the chapel and grounds. Councillor Sherrot said the ceremony had offended the town. In fact, very few Brighton people knew what had happened.

Today, the Aleister Crowley cult interests more people than it did in his lifetime. His books on what he called Magick, his novel *Moonchild* and his volume of 'Confessions', were not published in full until the late 1960s and have since become best sellers. At the same time, his experiences with hallucinatory drugs were of huge interest during the 'swingin' sixties'. The Beatles included a picture of Crowley on the sleeve of their massively popular LP disc, *Sgt. Pepper's Lonely Hearts Club Band*. If you've got a copy, see if you can find him – you know who he is now! A clue - he's in the back row.

Incidentally, it's not known what became of Crowley's ashes, following the cremation at Woodvale. They were last in the hands of the funeral directors, who supervised the cremation. A firm that unfortunately no longer exists...

'King Solomon'

The *Brighton Herald*, of 15th January 1955, devoted nearly a whole page to an article about the notorious 'King Solomon', whose house at 35 Carlton Terrace, Portslade, was about to be demolished. It said: 'There must be people still living who can recall the scandalous 'goings-on' at King Solomon's former headquarters in Edward Street, Brighton, the one-time Boss's Riding School and for many years now the Salvation Army Citadel.' This building is seen in the photograph.

The scandalous goings-on were 'religious' ceremonies - where those participating were usually naked - instigated by the so-called King Solomon, whose real name was James William Wood. He was born in Maresfield, near Uckfield in Sussex, emigrated to Australia for a while, then turned up at Brighton about 1886, establishing a cult known as 'The Army of the Lord' at the Edward Street premises. How Wood managed to get well-off people to donate substantial funds to the community he established (he and others lived in the building) is a mystery but the article states: 'Ritual dances in 'The Sanctuary' became notorious and led to frequent disturbances. Indeed, King Solomon more than once found it necessary to descend from his throne and ascend into the dock at Brighton Police Court.'

On one occasion, he was fined £5 for assaulting one of his 'elders', a man named Revilions who, earlier, had responded to 'an inspired message by the prophet' by selling his tailoring business and handing over the entire proceeds to Solomon's cause (over £300). Because of his 'donation', he was allowed to live in the Sanctuary with his wife and six children. The assault came when Solomon wanted the family to move out (he said they were 'full of devils'), an argument became a fight and the police were called.

The Salvation Army Citadel, Edward Street, as it was in 1962

When funds became low, Wood moved to Portslade, then to Upton Park, West Ham, for a while, before returning to Carlton Terrace, Portslade, where things carried on much as before – including the naked rituals. He sent out a large number of extraordinary messages and manifestos, claiming he'd been commanded from 'on high' to change the name of Brighton to 'Yattakah' and he was going to take over the Royal Pavilion for his work and rename it 'The Sanctuary of Jehovah.'

Wood died in February 1916 aged eighty-five at his Portslade home. The house was subsequently demolished – and it's bizarre that before Wood took it over in the 1890s, it was the HQ of the Portslade Conservative Club! The Edward Street building - last used by the Salvation Army - came down in the 1960s, for road widening.

Auguste Thommen

Coming more up to date now, a great story was reported in the Brighton papers during August 1968, about someone winning a substantial amount of money using marked cards at the casino at the Hotel Metropole, which had recently opened.

An American visitor - Auguste Thommen - saw where the cards were kept for blackjack and, at an opportune moment, quietly removed them. He went to the hotel's restaurant and with a pair of nail clippers, calmly snipped extremely tiny pieces off the cards in a way that would enable him to differentiate them later by sense of touch. In subsequent games, he'd won £595 before staff became suspicious. He was arrested, ended up in court, convicted and the fine he had to pay was... £100! Who said crime doesn't pay?

Camping Couple

Tea on the lawn!

Another 'stroppy Brighton' story of August 1969. Two 'enraged' tourists, Charles Newell and Ruth Oxenbury, who'd been turned away from the Sheepcote Valley camp site at Whitehawk because it was full, decided to pitch their tent on the only available site they could find! The photograph shows them calmly brewing tea on the traffic roundabout opposite the Palace Pier – it was much bigger then and covered in grass.

The Great Omani

And just to prove that all the great Brighton characters aren't from the distant past, the late Ron Cunningham, otherwise known as The Great Omani, was just the sort of eccentric performer Brighton people could take to their hearts – one of Brighton's very last, great, 'end-of-the-pier' showmen.

Born in Windsor, in July 1915, he was the son of a wine importer and went to public school at Sherborne in Dorest. He worked for the family business, but on the death of his father, it failed and was sold off. Due to a damaged heart, he couldn't get into the army during World War II and it was while browsing through a second-hand bookshop in Charing

The Great Omani performing his blindfold speedboat stunt, underneath the West Pier, in the early 1960s

Cross Road that he came across *The Secrets of Houdini* by J.C. Cannell. This was the book that inspired Ron into the world of stunts, illusions and escapology and, after experimenting mainly with underwater stunts, he made his first public appearance in 1950. For the rest of his life, he would earn his living in the most bizarre ways imaginable...

He worked locally at Bognor Regis performing tricks in a straitjacket chained and padlocked to the supports of the pier as the tide rose. On Brighton's West Pier, he became well known for eating light bulbs, jumping though open flames onto a bed of broken glass and – seen here - regularly taking a speedboat in and out of the pier's superstructure, while blindfolded. As a bonus, the sea was on fire too, so if he crashed, he'd be burnt alive.

In 1977 he famously marked the Queen's Silver Jubilee by performing a handstand on the cliff edge of Beachy Head, with a Union Jack between his toes. A famous quote of his was: 'People will always flock to see anybody likely to kill themselves.'

As he grew elderly, he'd often do 'sit down' stunts at his local pub - the Bedford Tavern - in Kemp Town. It was here that he performed his last escape in 2005 – releasing himself from handcuffs with both arms on fire with lighter fluid – it's a popular *YouTube* video on the Internet.

He died in Brighton in October 2007. His last request was for a trapdoor in the hearse at his funeral! He wrote a short poem, which was read out at the service:

They lay the Great Omani in his box,
They have done it up with nails not locks,
But at his funeral do not despair;
Chances are he won't be there.

2: Peculiar events and happenings

The next section details bizarre events and happenings in Brighton and Hove, some well known, but several appearing in print for the first time

Early Letter

Going right back in time, one of the earliest surviving letters mentioning Brighton dates from 22nd July 1736. It was written by the Rector of Buxted, the Reverend William Clarke, to a friend named Bowyer. The part that follows mentions the extremely low height of the town's buildings at this time:

'But though we may build castles in the air, I assure you we live here underground almost. I fancy the architects here, actually take the altitude of the inhabitants, and lost not an inch between the head and the ceiling, and then dropping a step or two below the surface; the second storey is finished something under twelve feet. I suppose this was a necessary precaution against storms, that a man should not be blown out of his bed into New England, Barbary or God knows where. But as the lodgings are low, they are cheap. We have two parlours, two bed chambers, pantry etc. for five shillings per week, and if you really will come down you need not fear a bed or proper dimensions.'

Five shillings would be 25p today! The good Reverend was right about the low buildings coming about as a safeguard against storms. In the early 1700s, two severe storms all but wiped Brighton off the map.

The New Ship Hotel

This obviously takes its name from the Old Ship Hotel, which to start with was just called The Ship. Its frontage and main entrance were originally in Ship Street itself, not on the seafront road as they are today. It changed to *Old* Ship because a rival hotel opened on the other side of the street (around the middle of the 1600s) calling itself the New Ship. Both proprietors didn't want patrons getting the two mixed up, so the earlier hotel was prefixed 'Old'. The picture opposite shows the hotel in the 1920s, before it was rebuilt in its present 'Tudor' style a decade later (they did the same with the King and Queen in Marlborough Place).

In October 1792 a party of thirty-seven elderly nuns turned up at the New Ship, having been driven by persecution from their convent in Lisle, northern France, during the French Revolution. They arrived by packet steamer, with only £30 between them. The Prince of Wales and Mrs Fitzherbert set up a subscription (fundraising) for their relief, which raised £100. The landlord, a Mr Balcombe, was hard pressed to accommodate them during their stay, however, because he could not persuade them to sleep two to a bed! The nuns stayed on in Britain and founded a new priory, which still exists today at Fernham, Oxfordshire. In the 1980s, veteran Brighton historian Cliff Edwards, travelled to St Mary's to see if the nuns knew about the 1790 incident. Not only did they know all the details, they still blessed the royal family each day with a special Domine Salvum Fac ('Lord Make Safe' – Psalm 69), in honour of the Prince's kindness, all those years ago.

And there's an amazing postscript to this tale. 1805, landlord Balcombe of the New Ship won a lottery prize of £20,000 (yes, there were lotteries two hundred years ago and £20,000 was an incredible sum of money to win) but he had to share his prize with sixteen other winners! Despite this money, he stayed on at the New Ship, as host, for several more years.

The New Ship Hotel in the 1920s

Rabbit on the Moon

One of the most bizarre of all superstitions from Brighton's past concerns the fear instigated in the town's fishermen by rabbits or hares – even just saying the words. Equally bad was the shape of a hare appearing on the moon. Even in the 1930s we learn that at meetings of a 'prominent Cruising Club in Sussex' the mention of the word rabbit would bring about 'an unholy uproar'.

But a rabbit on the moon?

At the time of a full moon, there appears on its surface a large, dark patch – or combination of patches - which curiously resembles a hare or rabbit. This had actually been noted in ancient times and gave rise to all manner of 'lunar-hare myths' mostly originating in Asia; moon gods were often represented by rabbits and hares in the past. Moon

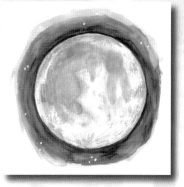

The hare appears on the moon

Brighton fishermen about to set sail

worship was common in all parts of the world, so much so that in Britain, in the seventh and eighth centuries, the Archbishops of Canterbury and York castigated all who did homage to the moon.

Whatever the origins, the sight of this hare on the moon meant that in Brighton – indeed all over Sussex - most fishermen would not set sail until later in the month as, for them, the hare had become an omen of ill-luck connected with witchcraft. If they did set sail, the belief was they might encounter a storm, their catch would be poor, or they might even be shipwrecked, so best to wait until the hare was, literally, 'phased out.'

There's a story told of two families of fisherfolk, who owned small luggers, and how they fell out. The row was a serious one causing, it's said, 'much bad blood'. One night, the men of the offended family got a rabbit skin and a pound of large iron tacks. They went to the boat belonging to the aggressors and nailed the skin – using all the tacks - to the mast in such a way that it would be a huge task to get it off again. This of course, would put the boat out of action till every scrap was removed, for no one would put to sea with even a shred of rabbit's skin on board.

So why were rabbits and hares – even just in outline – so feared and linked with witches?

Belief in witches was virtually absolute in the past. In Sussex there are any number of accounts of local witches supposedly transforming themselves into hares in order to get quickly from place to place to work their mischief and often being vigorously pursued by a crowd intent on killing the witch while in her 'alter-ego' state (in Dorset, apparently, in similar circumstances, only a pure, silver bullet would kill the hare).

A footnote to this story is that the author of this book climbed Chanctonbury Ring very recently – a noted centre for witchcraft in the past - and discovered a rough ring of stones near the famous circle of trees, surrounding a dead and rapidly decomposing hare. This could have been nothing, or could have been some modern-day occult ceremony involving a hare.

So we'll quickly move on!

West Street Post

Most people know about this post at the bottom of West Street (eastern side) that once stood with six others outside a fine house once on the site, bought in 1767 by an individual named Henry Thrale. It's seen below with the seven posts in front of it. Henry, along with his wife, Hester, moved in artistic and literary circles and invited many famous exponents in these areas to their West Street house. These included playwright Oliver Goldsmith (he wrote the play *She Stoops to Conquer*) diarist Fanny Burney, painter Joshua Reynolds and – one of the great characters of the period – Dr Samuel Johnson, the man responsible for the country's first proper, anecdotal dictionary (and brilliantly lampooned in an edition of TV's *Blackadder*).

The famous West Street post

Getting Johnson to stay at Brighton for any length of time was a near miracle as he hated the place, although he did enjoy riding through the Sussex countryside and attended church fairly regularly, but he found Brighton – a famous quote – 'so desolate, that if one had a mind to hang oneself for desperation at being obliged to live there, it would be difficult to find a tree on which to fasten the rope.'

The Thrale's house was demolished in 1866 and a large concert hall built on the site. This was a multi-purpose building and the Victorian's zeal for education saw many famous people

The Thrale's house in West Street

of the day giving lectures there, including H M Stanley (of 'Dr Livingstone, I presume?' fame) and the surgeon Frederick Treves, celebrated for his rescue of John Merrick ('The Elephant Man') and an appendix operation on Edward VII (Queen Victoria's son and successor); as Gypsy Lee predicted on page 37, this delayed his coronation in 1902 by several weeks.

The concert hall had a long and chequered history and was one of the first places in Brighton to show 'moving pictures' in the very early 1900s. It became

Samuel Johnson

the legendary dance hall Sherrys in 1919, which featured in Graham Greene's famous story, *Brighton Rock*. Sherrys closed in 1948 and the building served as a roller-skating rink, then bingo hall, before the frontage was rebuilt and the interior altered to make it the modern nightclub it is today. Outside, through all the many changes over the years, the single post from the Thrale's house has survived (by a miracle) and is the oldest part of West Street still standing.

Cliff Collapse

The cliffs in Black Rock area of Brighton and Hove have always been precarious and prone to crumbling away – even in modern times. In recent years a landslip resulted in the Asda supermarket car park at the Marina being closed when several tons of rubble fell on it – so nothing new!

On 30th July 1787, the *Sussex Weekly Advertiser*, the first local newspaper published in Sussex, reported the following bizarre incident:

'Early on Monday morning, as Mr Hart, milliner in Castle Square (Brighton) and Mr Stiles, hairdresser, of the same place, were riding home from Rottingdean, where they had been the preceding day on a visit to some friends, a sudden puff of wind took Mr Hart's hat from his head (within a quarter of a mile of Brighthelmston) and carried it a considerable distance from him, upon which he dismounted, and in attempting to recover his hat, went so near the brink of the cliff that a large portion of it gave way with him, and precipitated him with great violence to the beach below, whereby he received so much internal hurt that it proved mortal to him; but not immediately feeling the bad effects of it, he got up and walked to Brighthelmston, where, meeting his companion (who had jogged on with the horse, unknowing of the accident) he took the horse from him, and having led him to the stable, went home, where he languished till Wednesday, then expired, to the great grief of his family.'

Fish Wives to the Rescue!

Even though Brighton's fishermen were a thoroughly superstitious lot, they could be extremely stroppy - and so could be their wives and offspring! Again, in the old *Sussex Weekly Advertiser*, on the 15th October 1787, we read:

'Captain B----ll, who lately put the Brighthelmston fishermen under so much fear of being impressed in consequence of having hired a number of men, and given them the air of a press gang, was on Monday evening fairly put to the rout by the fishermen's wives and daughters, who assembled in a considerable body, armed with mops, besoms, firepans, etc. etc., and therewith pursued the captain so closely that he was obliged to

make his escape out of the windows of several houses in which he had taken shelter, and by means thereof, reached a post chaise and four that was provided for him, and thus escaped the fury of the victorious amazons, who then returned peaceably to their respective homes, to congratulate their husbands and their sweet hearts on their happy deliverance.'

A Brighton fishwife with her child

The Press Gang at Brighton

Another *Sussex Weekly Advertiser* item, of 11th September 1780, gives minimal details – perhaps wisely – of a truly ghastly incident involving the press gang and one man's efforts to escape being taken:

'Last Saturday one of the fishermen at Brighthelmstone on being impressed, attempted to cut off his left hand, to prevent his being sent on board a man-of-war, which he so nearly effected, that it was thought surgeon's assistance would be required to complete the amputation. He had been pressed before he made his escape.'

Yuk!

Wives for Sale

Now something very different. It's always said that Thomas Hardy, the well-known Dorset author, got his idea for the sale of a wife - which features in the opening scene of his 1886 novel *The Mayor of Casterbridge* - after witnessing such an event taking place at a Brighton market. This could have been in September 1874, when Hardy had just married in London and came to stay at Morton's Hotel, in Queen's Road, before embarking for Dieppe (from the Chain Pier) and his honeymoon in France. The weather wasn't good during Hardy's stay, but he and his wife Emma passed the time by visiting the pier and recently opened Aquarium, also attending a concert at the Royal Pavilion. Hardy had a swim in the sea, too, but found it very rough.

Strange as it seems, the selling of wives was a reasonably common practice in England between 1700-1880. One of the earliest recorded wife sales took place in Birmingham as far back as 1733. Here, reports relate how 'Samuel Whitehouse sold his wife, Mary Whitehouse, in open market, with all her faults, to Thomas

Thomas Hardy

Griffiths. Value, one guinea'.

Wives for sale were taken to the market with halters around their necks, just like livestock and had to stand on a stool or table, while 'bidding' took place. In fact, it seems most of them were there willingly and sales took place with the full agreement of both husband and wife. It was virtually impossible for ordinary folk in Britain to get divorced at this time, due to the costs involved, and wife selling was the 'quickie' divorce of the times; the authorities seem to have mostly turned a blind eye to it. Presumably it was done publicly, so the event was witnessed and people - including friends and family - would know of the new marital situation. Also, in the majority of cases, the wife was sold to an existing lover and the price had been agreed on by all parties beforehand. The 'bidding' – where seemingly anyone could join in – was largely sham and the announcement, 'Sold!' would be made when the new husband had shouted out the agreed price. By tradition, the husband would then use the money he got to buy drinks for everyone in the local inn - including his ex-wife and her new husband.

In Brighton we have several records of wife selling, but only sketchy details of what went on. The sales probably took place at the market building, then actually in Market Street, which stood until 1830; the Town Hall now occupies the site. In February 1799, a man named Staines sold his wife for five shillings, plus eight quarts of beer, to a James Marten. In May 1826 another wife was sold for a sovereign and four half crowns (equal to ten shillings). This woman had two children with her. The oldest stayed with the husband, the other - a baby - went with the mother and the new husband. A record of the transaction was duly written in the market ledger as just another sale. It's reported the woman was smiling and seemed perfectly happy with the new arrangement.

Wives for sale!

Smuggling at Hove

In the smuggling days of the eighteenth century, Preston, north of Brighton, was part of the parish of Hove. Church services were held at each on alternate Sundays. One Sunday, the vicar made a mistake and went to St Andrew's Church in Hove when he should have been at the Preston church. The verger stopped him from entering saying, 'You can't hold no service here, Pa'son.' When asked why, he was told, quite straight-faced, that, 'the church is full o' tubs and the pu'pit full o' tea!'

Dead and Buried – in the Lewes Road!

During the late Victorian period, fairs and travelling circuses were a customary feature of Brighton life. At one such fair, held regularly on open ground at the bottom of Bear Road, an elephant died and disposal of the remains presented quite a predicament. Eventually, a large pit had to be dug, which today would be at the northern junction of

Natal and Nesbitt Roads - site of a buried elephant!

Natal and Nesbitt Roads – then, of course, open fields. Any future redevelopment of the area requiring deep excavations might just uncover it! Headlines about an ancient mammoth being found off Lewes Road would probably be in all the local papers!

Bible Bullet

Private Hacket's life-saving Bible

There are lots of tales from World War I where soldiers carrying Bibles into battle were saved when a bullet struck them, preventing serious injury or even death. Well, here's a photograph that proves it was true for one man who ended up at a military hospital in Brighton. Most of the wounded British were sent back across the channel, then transported by train to various locations along the south coast, where emergency hospitals had been set up. In Brighton, the Brighton, Hove and Sussex Grammar School in Old Shoreham Road became

the Second General Eastern Hospital. It was here that Private William Hacket, of the 1st Worcestershire Regiment, arrived, having been wounded at Armentieres on August 20th 1915 (the date he gave doesn't quite tie up with the actual battle of Armentieres proper, which began in October). However, whenever he was wounded, the bullet passed through the outer cover of his Bible, then all the pages, stopping at the very last one. And, fortunately, we have this nice, clear photograph of it.

All-metal houses in Queen's Park Road

Metal Houses

It could only happen in Brighton! As an experiment, in 1922-23, these two houses were built entirely of metal in Queen's Park Road. Why? Due to the huge shortage of conventional building materials in the slump following World War I, it was decided to try out other means of house construction and the government funded half the cost of these two peculiar properties. As far as is known, they were completely unique to Brighton. Technically known as Weir Steel Homes, they lasted until 1969. Needless to say, they didn't catch on. Imagine the rain drumming on the roof!

The Viaduct Bomb

Brighton was hit by fifty-six air raids during World War II. The first was on 15th July 1940, the last on 22nd March 1944. 381 high explosive bombs were dropped on the town, with incendiary bombs – to start fires – too numerous to count. The air-raid sirens went off 1058 times. Civilian casualties were 988, with 198 killed, 357 seriously injured and 433 slightly injured. 5000 houses were damaged, with just over 200 having to be completely demolished. 894 were seriously damaged and 14,232 slightly damaged.

The bombed Brighton viaduct

It's generally reckoned the worst raid was on 14th September 1940 (a Saturday), when a single plane bombed the Kemp Town area. One bomb scored a direct hit on an Odeon Cinema in St George's Road, and in this building and surrounding streets, fifty-five people lost their lives in a matter of moments.

But not every bomb that fell went off. All over Brighton, indeed the whole country, many bombs failed to detonate and bounced about, ricocheted, turned somersaults and so on, all before coming to rest somewhere, ready for disposal teams to move in and make them safe.

A key target in Brighton was naturally the railway network and any bridge, cutting or tunnel associated with it. Accordingly, the viaduct over the London Road and the main Brighton terminus and its railway works close by were a high priority for the enemy to destroy.

This viaduct gives us Brighton's most bizarre bombing incident of the whole war. Twenty-five Focke-Wulf 190s descended onto the town on Tuesday 25th May 1943, from the southeast, and dropped over twenty bombs across a wide area. Twenty-four people would die, fifty-eight were seriously injured and 150 houses rendered uninhabitable in a matter of minutes. As the planes swept down, one eye-witness reported seeing a man on a roof, or at a high window, discharging a revolver at the planes, trying to bring one of them down.

The bomb that hit the railway viaduct spanning the London Road - the last to be dropped – performed an incredible sequence of acrobatics before detonating. It first hit a building in Campbell Road, then was deflected through a garden wall, bounced a couple of times in the road then passed through the front wall of 2 Argyle Villas. It travelled through two rooms in this house and out through a back window, still without going off. The bomb travelled a further sixty feet to a workshop, passed through its first floor, then travelled on to the railway viaduct striking one pillar, then another, before finally going off. The explosion dislodged the top portion of two arches, bringing down a mass of bricks and debris, but leaving the railway lines intact, still spanning the gap.

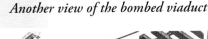

Another view of the bombed viaduct

Equally breathtaking was how quickly the break was repaired and within days trains were using the viaduct again.

The White Street Bomb

Following the Kemp Town bombing, on Wednesday 18th September, at 8.17 pm, the Edward Street area was attacked, with White Street receiving a direct

White Street bombed

hit. Several people at 2, 4, 5 and 6 were killed, as was a seventy-two year-old woman living at 5 Blaker Street, the next street up. At number 6 itself, five members of a family named Tucker – including a nine-month-old baby – were all killed, the house completely destroyed and a large crater left in the road.

Two bombs were dropped and their impact was staggering. The wheels of a mangle in one of the White Street houses ended up embedded in a roof in the next street. The second bomb - that fell on a builder's yard in neighbouring Mighell Street - flung a massive iron girder, twelve feet long and weighing two hundredweight over the rooftops into White Street, a distance of some seventy-five yards. From the same workplace, a wheelbarrow was also blown over the White Street roof line, a distance of more than 300 yards.

The mummified hand

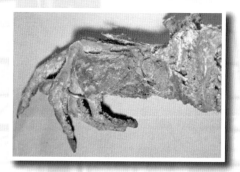

The truly bizarre part of this ghastly bombing incident was that one of the Tucker family at no 6 – female - was, quite literally, blown to pieces, and her left hand shot across the street and lodged itself in the eaves of the house directly opposite. There it stayed for many years, becoming semi-mummified – as seen in the picture. When discovered, it was identified from a ring on one of the fingers. The White Street houses were rebuilt after the war, in a different style to those of the rest of the street and, in September 1953, the author of this book was born at no. 6, where the Tucker family had once lived.

The First Brighton Festival

More cheerful matters now. Those organising the initial Brighton Festival could hardly have foreseen the huge event it would escalate to and it remains one of the most important developments of 1960's Brighton. The first festival ran from 14th – 30th April 1967 and had an 'all seeing- eye' as its logo, seen on the flags in the picture here, being set up on the traffic roundabout near the Palace Pier.

A stunt of the first festival that famously backfired was an ambitious plan to 'paint' a huge Union Jack on the surface of the sea between the piers. 'I want to stress that this is an experiment,' said Ian Hunter, the festival's director. In hindsight, there are many other words that would be appropriate!

Festival flags in the Steine

In the picture below, well-known local fisherman Alan Hayes is out in his launch, *Fair Chance*, with artist William Mitchell and assistants, planning to put the special dye onto the sea. The plan for a Union Jack had to be scrapped, as the dyes needed were unavailable, so the idea was just to change the colour of the sea. 'The only effect', wrote the *Argus*, was large splodges of fluorescent sickly green, which lasted more than an hour, discolouring the briny.'

Alan Hayes filled in the detail: 'They arrived with a spray gun and two five-gallon drums of very concentrated crystals. Turning into the wind, the boat hit a wave and a cup of crystals flew into the air, covering the crew. Spray hit them and they all turned green.'

'I feel it has been an interesting interlude in the festival events,' William Mitchell said afterwards. He was also working on a sculpture, *The Spirit of Brighton*, to stand in the Churchill Square development.

There were a number of examples of what was known as 'concrete poetry' displayed around the town during this first festival. It was presumed that this meant poetry that existed in some other form other than on paper.

The painting-the-sea stunt

So words, groups of words or two or three lines of words appeared at random round the town, at best amusing, at worst totally obscure in meaning. There was even a raft, moored a quarter of a mile out at sea, between the piers, which had three pylons on it bearing the words

'LOVE', 'PASSION' and 'BEAUTY' in large letters. Constant movement and spray dislodged them after a while until they seemed about to wilt completely. 'All passion bent' was a remark heard from one onlooker.

The last of the quirkier events was a 'Bonfire of Vanities' on the beach. People were encouraged to come and throw anything they considered ugly into the flames. There were many outrageous suggestions, of course, but few actual offers; the event literally fizzled out.

Despite all this, the first Brighton Festival was judged to be a huge success; an extraordinary new era in Brighton's artistic fortunes had begun.

Brighton has such a rich and diverse heritage, almost any area of human activity or pioneering endeavour can be found somewhere in its past. Early theatre and cinema, inventions, crime, transport, literature, mysteries - you name it, it's there. So too is the highly serious business of what might be called 'pulling a fast one' - in other words jokes and hoaxes - and what follows remain two of the best.

Harry Bensley

This story of the eccentric Mr Bensley has been a long-standing mystery which resurfaces every so often, but its authenticity has never really been resolved - until now. Well, kind of. Did he walk round the world with his pram for a bet, or didn't he? Thanks to the wonders of the Internet and communication with his descendants, it's now possible to determine more of the truth behind his legendary story. Again, though, you'll have to wait till the end to see the Brighton and Hove connection.

The story – as usually told – is that in the early 1900s, an age of silly bets and wagers, John Pierpont Morgan, the famous American millionaire and Hugh Cecil Lowther, Lord Lonsdale, known as the 'Sporting Peer' (the Lonsdale belt in boxing is named after him), were debating – at a London 'gentleman's club' - whether it was possible for a man to walk round the world without showing his face. Lonsdale believed that it could be done, but Morgan didn't. They agreed on a wager of £21,000 (about £1½ million today) and offered the task to a 31 year-old, prosperous 'playboy' called Harry Bensley. He accepted, despite many extremely bizarre rules that were drawn up.

Bensley would have to push a pram all the way, wearing an iron mask, which was not to be taken off for any reason. He had to begin with only £1 in his pocket and a single change of underwear in the pram! He had to pass through a long list of towns in England and Wales and 125 towns in 18 other countries, which would take him to every continent except Antarctica! He also had to find himself a wife (who was not to see his face, remember) and make money by selling picture postcards of himself (like the one here). To make sure he followed all these rules, a man was paid to escort him.

This was some bet!

But Harry cheerfully set off from Trafalgar Square wearing his 4½lb. iron helmet and pushing his pram on 1st January 1908. He met up with King Edward VII at the Newmarket races and sold him a postcard for £5 (he wouldn't give the King his autograph though), but at Bexleyheath, Kent, he was arrested for selling his cards without a licence. He was ordered to remove his mask by the court magistrate, but when the stunt was explained, he was allowed to keep it on and only fined 2/6d. He was also in Wiltshire, Hampshire and Sussex (note the card here is signed from Brighton on 11th February (?) 1909 – although this isn't really the Brighton connection, which comes later.

In six years – so the story goes - Bensley pushed his pram across twelve countries receiving 200 offers of marriage on the way – some from titled ladies! He declined them all. He was in Italy in August 1914 and had only six more countries to visit when World War I broke out. He felt it his duty to join the army, so the bet was called off. A consolation prize of £4000 from J.P. Morgan was given to charity. Bensley served in the British army in the first year of the War, was wounded and eventually invalided out in 1915. Bensley had been pretty well off, but he lost most of his money during the Russian Revolution when investments he had there became worthless and he was left destitute. After the war, Bensley moved to live in Wivenhoe, Essex with his wife Kate (possibly married to her as early as 1898). He worked in low-key jobs like cinema doorman and YMCA warden, but became elected twice as a local councillor for the Labour Party. According to one report, during the Second World War, Bensley was a bomb checker at an ammunition factory. The Brighton connection comes right at the tail end of the story - Harry Bensley died in a bed-sit at 42 Riley Road on May 21, 1956. His death certificate confirms this.

Harry Bensley with his trademark iron helmet and pram

42 Riley Road

That's more or less how the great legend goes. An amazing story and, like most legends, there's some truth to it, but an awful lot of embellishment, particularly once the epic journey gets underway.

The real story goes much more like this. Firstly, the journey wasn't so much a bet as a kind of penalty. In an article in *The Times* in January 2008, marking the day – a hundred years previously, that the stunt began - Bensley's granddaughter, Kim McNaught, said that her father had tracked Bensley down to a hospital in Brighton in 1956, only months before he died aged seventy-nine. He was already very ill and confided the truth about the famous wager; 'He said it was not a bet, it was a forfeit. He had bet a great deal of money on a hand of poker, having made out that he had a big estate in Ireland and money in Russia. When he lost, he was told he would have to go to jail or take a forfeit, and that was to go around the world in an iron mask. It was a punishment.'

Hard on the heels of Harry has been Geoffrey Corfield of Ontario in Canada, who has made finding out what really happened something of a life work. Mr Corfield agrees that while the first part of the trip can be confirmed – although the sitings could still have been staged – he feels the way the whole bet was set up is, in itself, highly doubtful. He has trawled through the J.P. Morgan Company archives, the Pierpont Library, and a biography on Morgan by writer Jean Strouse, which involved fifteen years of research, none making any link at all between Morgan and a man named Harry Bensley.

America would have loved an eccentric like Harry Bensley. But there isn't a single mention of him in any American newspaper for the first six months of 1908, with May and June the time he should really have been there. Nor is he in any newspaper of any other country abroad. In fact he probably never went anywhere except southern Britain, which begs the question, just where was he for most of the six year stunt? This really isn't known – yet!

J.P. Morgan died in March 1913; he's meant to have paid Harry's £4000 compensation in 1914. Obviously he couldn't have done this, but his son might have, Jack Morgan. However, there's no mention of Harry in any of his surviving correspondence either.

As for the offers of marriage – all two hundred of them (!) – it's believed Bensley had secretly married a housemaid called Mabel Reed, soon after starting the journey; he kept the marriage secret because he had been released from jail only recently for another, bigamous marriage. Quite a lad, our Harry!

Sadly, the great stunt of a marathon round the world runs out of steam when the modern-day research piles up against it. It clearly didn't happen but we're still left with one of the great hoaxes – or part hoaxes - of Edwardian times.

Now, the only real mystery left is... where's the mask and that pram?

Paddy's Prank

Another great joke happened more recently – it's nice they still do! Back in October 1963, a black Cadillac pulled up outside the Royal Pavilion in Brighton and a young Arab gentleman stepped out, dressed in full headdress and flowing robes, accompanied by a private secretary and travel aide. This was Prince Emir Khalid ibn Abdul Asir ibn Saud, fourth son of King Saud of Arabia, who was courteously greeted by the Pavilion's director, Clifford Musgrave, then given a guided tour of the building, as was usual with all VIPs visiting Brighton and wanting to see the famous Brighton palace. Tea and polite conversation followed in the Committee Room.

Suitably impressed and pleased with the cordiality of his reception, the Prince made his farewells, returned to his car and was driven away. Nothing seemed wrong - just another dignitary making a visit - until local papers appeared later in the day exposing the whole thing as a hoax. 'Paddy's Prank' (as it became known) had been thought up by a nineteen-year-old building student, Patrick Cook, from Brighton College of Technology. He'd spent three months in the Middle East studying architecture and had bought the robe and headdress there. His understanding of Arabic was good enough to reply to a completely off the cuff remark made by one of the Pavilion's attendants. Later, Musgrave and others present

The sheikh arrives!

said they knew it was a hoax (we'll believe him!), but went along with it as it would have been, 'a pity to spoil the perpetrator's fun when they had gone to such great trouble, and the history of the Royal Pavilion would not be complete without an event like this once in a while.'

3: Weird methods of transportation

Daddy-long-legs Railway

Next, a short section on what can only be described as bizarre methods of transportation!

Volk's Electric Railway has seen well over a century and a quarter of service on Brighton seafront since opening in 1883. But Volk built another railway, that ran over the sea, long since gone.

This was the extraordinary vehicle seen in the old photographs here, resembling a tramcar on legs, which could be found on Brighton's eastern beaches between 1896 and 1901. It took visitors from the Banjo Groyne to Rottingdean and back, via a seabed trackway, some three miles in length.

At high tide the ride was at its most exhilarating, although the speed was comparatively slow at about six miles an hour. Passengers embarked from a specially-built pier adjoining the Banjo Groyne; the journey cost a shilling return (5p today) and depending on the sea conditions, took about thirty-five minutes each way.

And what powered this contraption through the water? Would you believe it was electricity?!

Brighton inventor and engineer Magnus Volk masterminded this incredible venture. The son of a German clockmaker and a child prodigy, Magnus enjoyed experimenting with electrical gadgets from an early age. In his late twenties he equipped his house (40 Preston Road) with the first domestic electric light in

The Brighton & Rottingdean Seashore Electric Railway at the Banjo Groyne

the town and set up his own telephone system. In 1883 he successfully installed electric lighting inside the Royal Pavilion.

Also in 1883, Volk began running the well-known electric railway that still operates along Madeira Drive, now listed in the *Guinness Book of Records* as the oldest electric railway in the world. This originally ran only a short distance along the seafront, but due to its immense popularity with visitors, was extended in 1884 to the Banjo Groyne (where the sheds for the railway are today). It was then that Volk conceived adding a completely different railway – originally known as 'The Brighton & Rottingdean Seashore Electric Railway' - so that people could travel on to reach Ovingdean and Rottingdean. He was partnered on this project by engineer Richard St George Moore, who would design the Palace Pier a few years later.

Pioneer setting off for Rottingdean

The vehicle Volk designed for the passengers resembled something out of a Jules Verne fantasy. Part pier, part tram, part boat, it was made at Gloucester, at the railway works there, and would be given the name *Pioneer*. It weighed fifty tons, the legs were twenty-eight feet long and the deck was forty-six feet by thirty-two. There was room for 150 passengers 'on board'. The electricity, providing the driving power, came from a generator under a short pier built at Rottingdean, the eastern terminus for the railway, and this was fed along cables held up by posts situated alongside the track. Two 'arms' similar to those on a trolley bus, conveyed the power to the car (these can just be seen in the photograph above).

When everything had been built and installed, a very serious ceremony was carried out by the Board of Trade, to see if the railway was safe enough for public use. *Pioneer* was first run at high tide, through some fifteen feet of water, then later, at low tide, where all manner of obstacles were placed on the track – iron bars, lumps of rock, and huge pieces of timber – to see if they would be pushed aside or not. Of course they were and the railway was inaugurated on 28th November 1896 and opened to the public on the 30th.

However, only a few days later, one of the biggest storms ever to hit Brighton descended on 4th December. This was the great storm that took away the Chain Pier and wrecked virtually everything along the promenade, including both of Volk's railways. The short embarkation pier built out from the Banjo Groyne, was severely damaged, the vehicle itself overturned and it looked like the end of the line for Volk's bold new venture.

Not a bit of it. Volk was nothing if not dogged in his approach to adversity. He quickly repaired everything, although simplified the design of the pier, and within a few months, the Brighton & Rottingdean Seashore Electric Railway was up and running again, reopening in July 1897. The public soon nicknamed the

Some of the surviving blocks the railway ran along

vehicle, 'Daddy-long-legs', because of its resemblance to a large spider.

On February 20th 1898, the railway carried its most famous passenger, the Prince of Wales, eldest son of Queen Victoria, later King Edward VII. He rode with the Duke and the Duchess of Fife, who lived on the seafront at Kemp Town. The Duchess was his daughter. A suitable plaque commemorating royal patronage was fixed inside the saloon.

The sheer originality of the railway attracted massive interest; even *The New York Herald* got to hear of it and commented: 'Mechanically, and as a seashore novelty, it beats anything yet done by us inventive Yankees.'

It's sad to relate that the railway was forced to close after only four years of operation. The Brighton Corporation decided to repair and extend the groynes on the beaches at Black Rock, which had become extremely dilapidated at this time. To continue the service, Volk would have had to divert his line further out to sea, which would have made the ride even more thrilling, but ultimately would have been impractical. As compensation, he was allowed to extend his original electric railway to Black Rock, which is still its destination today.

Many of the blocks the seashore railway ran on are still in place and can be seen (and climbed on) at low tide, well east of the Marina. Nothing else remains, although a film sequence taken of the railway operating has recently been discovered.

Although in its day the railway ride was seen as a fascinating and quaint novelty, the plain fact is it was an extremely audacious amenity on a par with the plan to put a

Original poster for the Daddy-long-legs

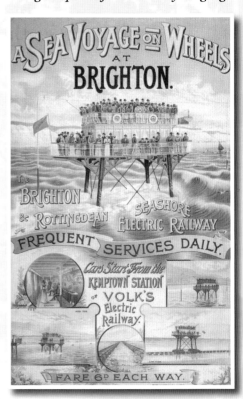

monorail along Brighton and Hove seafront today. Was it as controversial? Of course it was, particularly with the horse-cab operators and those who ran pleasure boat trips from the eastern beaches, who thought it would take their trade away (they thought this about Volk's electric trains too, when they first started running). And we can only wonder what the good residents of Kemp Town thought, having such a strange and perhaps 'cheap' amusement on their doorsteps.

Whatever anyone thought, one thing remains hard fact; Magnus Volk's Brighton & Rottingdean Seashore Electric Railway was the most bizarre seaside novelty ride ever devised. And somehow, you feel it could only have happened at Brighton!

Brighton's Bubble!

Moving on in time, one of the quirkiest cars ever seen on the roads of Britain was the three or four-wheeled Isetta, better known as the 'Bubble Car'.

Local interest is that, although designed in Italy, they were manufactured from 1957 in part of the old railway locomotive works located in New England Street, Brighton. The production firm was managed by ex-BOAC pilot, R. J. Ashley, with ninety cars a week initially being made. Output soon rose to over two hundred 'Bubbles' coming off the line each week, involving a staff of 250 workers. Each car took a maximum of just sixteen hours to produce, including twenty minutes in the paint shop. Today, the factory site lies under the New England Quarter housing estate, off the London Road.

In 1961 the popularity of the car saw BMW take over production and the works moved to Victoria Road, Portslade, where assembly continued until 1964. Some 30,000 'Bubble Cars' were produced in all.

In a *Brighton and Hove Gazette* of February 1962, a detailed report on the cars was given. The price locally was £320/9/- for the standard saloon, £356/1/1 for what was called the Plus model. Both these were of the three-wheel type and gave sixty to seventy miles a gallon. Top speed was just over 50 mph. Having only three wheels, a driving licence wasn't needed, only one for a motorcycle. The turning circle required was twenty-five feet and they would fit any garage as the height was only 4ft 4½ ins, the length 7 ft 6ins.

'From the very start,' the

Brighton's own Bubble Car

At the wheel

report informed readers, 'the Isetta is unconventional. To get in you do not go to the side of it but to the front where the door opens forwards, being hinged on the right. Open it by turning the lever on the right-hand side and it swings outwards, the steering wheel swinging with it to make access easier for the driver. It is easier for the driver to get in first and passengers afterwards, but when getting out the driver should leave last. Controls are fairly conventional, with the clutch pedal on the left of the foot of the steering column, the footbrake pedal, operating hydraulically on all three wheels, on the right of the column and the accelerator pedal on the extreme right.'

But it's hard to know what to make of changing gear 'with or without the use of the clutch' and the operation would go 'with a bang.' The report also said that when road-testing the Isetta, 'over poor surfaces the ride is a little harsh.'

In January 1967, an accident occurred involving a 'Bubble' that hit the headlines. Lily Flynn, who lived in McWilliam Road, Woodingdean, died in the Royal Sussex County Hospital, Kemp Town, after being struck by one near the Downs Hotel. Why this fatality caused such attention was because she was the mother of screen idol Errol Flynn, the legendary Hollywood film star; understandably, questions were raised about the safety of the new vehicles.

But what happened to all the thousands of 'Bubbles' produced over forty years ago? Where are they today? The one seen here, looking as good as the day it came off the construction line (in 1963), belongs to Jeff Wareing, secretary of the Isetta Owner's Club of Great Britain, a thriving group with some 450 members. It's safely housed at his home in Marus Bridge, Wigan, and still driven and exhibited at various rallies throughout the year. The club has a website and lively newsletter, where various other Isettas can be seen, including some highly 'customised' versions. The website even has a cut-out,

View from the rear!

cardboard model of an Isetta you can print off and assemble - if you'd like an Isetta of your own! However, the main purpose of the group, as you'd imagine, is to ensure parts and spares are available, to keep the old vehicles going. It was this club that presented a plaque to commemorate the site of the old Isetta factory, unveiled in June 2003 by an old employee, Leonard White; this date also commemorated fifty years of the car and twenty-five years of the Club.

Brighton has always been at the forefront of ingenious transport innovations – there were also the trams, both of Volk's Railways, and the 'wing and a prayer' aeroplanes that buzzed the town during the early years of Shoreham airport. It should be no surprise then, that this imaginative, if idiosyncratic little car is their modern counterpart – and those who still own one won't have a harsh word said about them!

4: Murderous, grisly and scary tales

Now let's change tack completely and have a few grisly, macabre stories, all true, the sort that make good bedtime reading! First, a famous murder...

The Holloway Murder

A really grisly Brighton murder came to light in July 1831, during the early reign of William IV. The body of a woman, minus head, arms and legs, was found in a hole dug at a copse near the railway embankment at Lover's Walk, Preston. Soon afterwards, the missing head and limbs were found in 'a privy' in Margaret Street.

John Holloway

This is the well-known Holloway case, retold many times, where pregnant Celia Holloway was strangled in 'Donkey Row' (later Sun Street, at the bottom of Edward Street) by her husband John, chopped up and disposed of. He was assisted by Ann Kennett, who he was having an affair with, the pair of them living at Margaret Street; Holloway enticed Celia to Donkey Row on the pretext they were going to live there together.

It didn't take long for the authorities to put two and two together and Holloway and Kennett were put on trial. He maintained he was innocent all through the proceedings, but was found guilty and publicly hanged at Horsham in December 1831 before a huge crowd; Kennett had been found not guilty earlier, when the trial first came to an assize court.

But the murder or hanging isn't the reason the Holloway murder features in this book. It was immediately *after* the hanging we get the really bizarre parts. Here's how the newspapers of the time reported the first weird incident...

'After the body had hung about a quarter of an hour, a man ascended the scaffold

Holloway and Kennett dismember the corpse

with the executioner and, seating himself on its edge, took off his hat. The hangman then loosened Holloway's hands, the palms of which he rubbed on the forehead of the person, who, we observed, was afflicted with a wen, which he superstitiously supposed would be cured by the process, for which he paid 2s and 6d'.

A wen was the word then – usually – for a cancerous growth on the scalp.

We learn that the Under Sheriff, who was presiding over the execution, would not allow any further similar actions until after the body had been cut down – perhaps there was a queue of people wanting wens and other eruptions 'cured'.

The noose was sold off to a young man from Lewes, and Holloway's body was taken to the Town Hall at Brighton and put on public show! 'Many thousands of persons' lined up to see the body (23,000 in all – someone must have counted them!), before it was handed over to the county hospital 'where after dissection, a skeleton will be formed of the bones.'

The remains of Celia Holloway were buried in St Peter's Church, Preston (the one near Preston Manor) and there's still a plaque on the wall that records the crime.

The memorial plaque to Celia Holloway in St Peter's churchyard

Grave Robbing

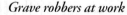

Grave robbers at work

In the early 1800s many people feared the activities of grave robbers who stole the bodies of the recently buried. The body snatchers were known as 'resurrection men'. Some were looking for valuables, which might have been buried with the corpses, but most stole bodies to supply doctors interested in dissecting them to further their knowledge of human anatomy.

Two men named Williamson and Bishop were hanged in 1831 for grave robbing. We know that in 1820, it was this same Williamson that removed at least one body from a grave in Brighton's St Nicholas churchyard, then the

St Nicholas Church, Brighton

only cemetery in the town.

The practice was widespread and different means were used to thwart the activities of the grave robbers. They included delaying burial by interring bodies in back gardens or in cellars until the corpses were no longer in a suitable state for anatomical research, mounting 'watchers' (sometimes armed) to guard recently buried bodies, or enclosing graves with anti-bodysnatching railings or grilles. In 1830, a Brighton firm named Duplocks, advertised 'metallic coffins' which, they claimed, 'would foil the efforts of any body snatcher'.

The Anatomy Act of 1832 allowed the bodies of workhouse paupers to be used for anatomical research and this reduced the activities of body snatchers to a large extent.

Christiana Edmunds

This woman, born in Brighton in 1829, lived with her widowed mother in lodgings at 16 Gloucester Place, Brighton (now demolished – where the old Astoria cinema stands). Across the road and further south

16 Gloucester Place up for sale in the early 1930s, prior to demolition for the building of the Astoria cinema

was the surgery of Dr Charles Beard at 64 Grand Parade (now beneath Brighton University's art faculty); a married man, but not disinclined to some mild flirtation. In 1869 Christiana fell in love with him, and secret, romantic letters followed. However, it all began to get a bit out of hand and Beard wrote: 'This correspondence must cease, it is no good for either of us'. Christiana upped the bar slightly by deciding to get rid of Mrs. Beard. She visited her with a gift of poisoned chocolates and the next day Mrs Beard fell ill. She recovered and Dr Beard had his suspicions about the chocolates - but at the time kept them to himself!

Her attempts to seduce Dr Beard having largely failed, Christiana, clearly mortified, decided to wreak revenge on anyone and everyone by buying chocolate creams from Maynards, the well-known confectioners (then at 39-41 West Street), and lacing them with strychnine. She boldly returned them to the unwary shopkeeper, on the pretence she 'didn't like them' and wanted to chose something different. He, of course, returned them to the jar or box and subsequently sold them on to the unsuspecting public ! The strychnine came from Isaac Garret, chemist, of 10 Queen's Road, Brighton, Christiana saying she needing to poison stray cats (Mr Garret told her she was being cruel), and when this excuse was exhausted she managed to get a neighbour to get the stuff for her and sign the poison book. As she herself couldn't keep appearing in Maynard's premises, small boys were pressed into service to buy the chocolate creams and she got them to return them too, exactly as she had done earlier.

How many did she poison? Well, probably quite a few, but in June 1871 Sidney Albert Barker, a four-year-old boy on holiday in Brighton with his parents, died after eating a chocolate bought at the shop. The Brighton Coroner, David Black, solicitor of 58 Ship Street, Brighton, held an inquest but the jury – bizarrely - returned a verdict of death by misadventure!

Maynard's in West Street – the 'scene of the crime'

She seemed to be getting away with it – so Christiana stepped up her campaign. She sent parcels to prominent people of Brighton containing poisoned cakes, sweets and fruit, which frequently made them ill, and it was only then that it dawned on people there was a poisoner on the loose. Panic and fear gripped Brighton as to where they would strike next. It was a typical Victorian melodrama being acted out on the streets of the town! Christiana cleverly sent parcels to herself, declaring that she too had been ill, but at this point Dr Beard finally told the police about his earlier suspicions. Her arrest followed and she was charged with the attempted murder of Mrs Beard. When she came to trial though, at the Old Bailey in London in January 1872, it was solely for the murder of little Sidney Miller (the case was transferred from the Sussex courts as it was thought a local trial might be prejudicial against her). She was found guilty and sentenced to death. She pleaded she was pregnant, but this was refuted by police doctors. During the trial, her mother gave details of a long history of insanity in the family on both sides, and the newspapers thought she was mad. Her death sentence was changed to life imprisonment and she died in Broadmoor Prison for the Criminally Insane in September 1907, aged seventy-eight. While confined, some romantic letters were intercepted, sent to the chaplain of Lewes Prison, causing Dr William Orange, Broadmoor's senior doctor to comment: 'she deceives for the pure love of deception'.

There's a postscript to this story. It's generally thought the Edmunds' case was the first trial witnessed by the great English barrister Sir Edward Marshall Hall. He would later make himself a household name by taking on the defence in a number of very famous English murder trials, earning himself the title of 'The Great Defender'. A Brighton resident, like Edmunds herself, he was just thirteen at the time of the trial; not when it was at the Old Bailey, but when it first came up at the Sussex assize hearings – it's known he attended. Perhaps Edmunds' bizarre case so enthralled him, he decided to make the law his career. After all, she was, in her way, one of the first women serial killers in history. Who knows?

House of Skulls

More 'wall of skulls' really, as seen in the photograph. This is truly one of the most bizarre tales in the whole book.

It goes like this. In the early part of Queen Victoria's reign (so let's say about 1845), a man named Cheeseman had a large workshop in Robert Street (or bordering onto it), possibly even a small factory, where a major accident took place involving nine fatalities. It's generally thought some kind of explosion took place, possibly a boiler detonating. Nothing *too* unusual about that. Accidents were common in Victorian factories and there were few health and safety regulations at this time. However, it's how the bodies were found that turns the story from the fairly ordinary to the downright creepy. They should have been found here, there and everywhere, grossly mutilated, but they were actually found lying almost in a perfect circular fashion, arms at sides, eight with their heads pointing towards the centre of the ring, feet pointing away, though the ninth had his head the other way, upside to the rest. They were all, largely, unharmed.

The wall of skulls, Robert Street

Then it gets creepier. Cheeseman decided to create a memorial to the men that died and put into the rebuilt exterior wall nine miniature skulls, eight the right way up, the ninth, as can be clearly seen in the photo, upside down. There was no plaque giving details of the accident, or who the men were. Just the skulls.

The ninth skull caused some consternation apparently, even in the so-called 'enlightened' Victorian times, as the depiction of an upside down man was – and still is - a potent symbol in witchcraft.

The wall survived until 1934 – when the photograph was taken – then was cleared for an extension to the printing works of Southern Publishers – home of the *Argus*, *Brighton Herald* and *Brighton and Hove Gazette* newspapers.

Just before the wall went, the *Gazette* reported : 'We are informed that the piece of wall containing the carvings is to be preserved and built into the new wall to be created on the site.'

So, at a later date, did some innocent *Argus* reporter have their desk in an office where one of the walls had the skulls preserved in it? Doubtful... but you never know! Could still be there, in the present building!

5: Extraordinary ghost stories

And finally, as Brighton and Hove is probably the most haunted city in the whole of Britain, we have to include a few really good ghost stories – the first one is the classic ghost story of old Brighton, but it's followed by some that aren't generally known...

Strike-a-light

East Street, almost certainly the city's oldest thoroughfare, can claim Brighton's best ghost story, a genuine shocker, which took place in an inn on the eastern side of the street, near the seafront end, called the Rising Sun (demolished in the 1860s). A suitably stormy night on Brighton beach, about 1760, starts the story, when local fisherman Swan Jervoise was bringing his boat ashore with a good catch of herring. He noticed some brilliant flashes coming from windows of the Rising Sun, which should have been closed, so while his crew dealt with the boat and fish, he made his way to the inn to investigate. At the door he heard striking noises, flint against steel, like a tinderbox being used, only far louder, and the great flashes from the windows were bright enough to light up the street. He hammered on the door, expecting the landlord, whom he knew, to open it and explain what was going on. Instead, the door swept back revealing a hideous, seven-foot tall

Strike-a-light appears to Jervoise

apparition, with staring grey eyes set in a white face. The figure was wearing a black cloak and a tall, white, pointed hat. This was the ghost known as 'Strike-a-light', who swept past Jervoise, out into East Street and was lost in the night.

The fisherman dissolved into hysterics, bringing the landlord to the door, who sat Jervoise by the still-glowing fire and gave him some ale. Left alone, he was just starting to recover his wits, when he felt a presence in the room. Turning, he was appalled to find the ghastly, towering creature had returned and was stood pointing fixedly at the fire with a bony finger. Jervoise fainted, was found by the landlord and put to bed. A priest named Father Anselm arrived the following morning to minister to Jervoise, and was duly told how the spectre's gaze was focused on the fireplace. Jervoise then slumped back and died. The fireplace was duly searched and the hearthstone prised up. Underneath was found a hoard of treasure - a huge number of gold coins. This caused excavations to be made in the inn's ancient cellars (in case there was any more to be found), but only some old bones were unearthed, along with an ancient sword. The bones were reburied in the local churchyard, at which point no more was heard of Strike-a-light, his apparent task, to alert someone to the treasure's hiding place, finally achieved. But what happened to the horde of treasure? Some sources say it went to a priory in Lewes, others that it went overseas.

An Untold Tale of Old Hove

St Andrew's Church

The next ghostly tale involves St Andrew's Church in Hove and first appeared in a magazine called *The Christian Spectator* in 1860, told by a priest named Chalcas. It's never appeared in any book before, as far as is known.

A policeman was on duty at two o'clock on a clear, moonlit night in Medina Villas. Nobody was about – as would be expected - when a somewhat agitated old man appeared and approached the policeman, asking the way to Hove Church. He had long hair and the appearance of 'a seafaring person.' 'I thought that a very strange question to be asking at that time of night,' the policeman later related, when recalling the story and, his suspicions aroused, offered to escort the man there, to see what he'd get up to. The old man didn't seem too happy about this, but conceded and together they approached the church. The gate was locked and the man – again displaying some anxiety - said he must get inside, so the policemen helped him climb over, but followed at a distance.

'My notion was,' he recollected, 'that either the old gentleman was wrong in the head and that I should not have too much trouble in leading him away after a bit, or else that he was a thief hiding spoons perhaps, and there again I was ready for him, for I had a revolver in my pocket.'

The man knocked on the church door – there was no answer, of course - so he walked round the back of the church, the policeman settling himself among some

Where the steps leading underground were!

tombstones, some ten yards from where the man was. He observed him go down some steps, 'as if to the church vaults', until out of sight. Then a conversation was heard, that couldn't be made out, except for one part, where the man said, 'Why don't you do it? Why don't you do it?' To which a woman answered, 'I will do it, I will do it.' Then he emerged, back up the steps, and the policemen was startled to see the man had a strange glowing light, circular in shape, below his chin, which faded away fairly quickly.

'I went up to him directly,' recalled the policeman, 'just where he stood, expecting to see the area where he had gone down by the steps – and there wasn't any there! The ground was made up close to the church wall and not in the least disturbed.' When asked about it, the man stood 'leaning with his arm on a high tombstone' and babbled about his life, saying he had communication with one who knew all about the other world. He said he now lived for these things, because he was sure they were true.

How the incident ended and how the two parted isn't recorded, but the old man was probably left to go on his way, climbing back over the wall, leaving the mystified policeman still staring at the ground where the phantom steps had been.

The Angels of Mons

Now a very famous ghostly sighting in Belgium, but involving local men.

As related in the 'bullet in the Bible' story on page 55, during World War I most of the British wounded in France were sent back across the Channel to various locations along the south coast where emergency hospitals had been set up. In Brighton, among the first three hundred

Soldier patients in the grounds of the school

to arrive were men of the 2nd Royal Sussex Regiment, who were nursed at the Second General Eastern Hospital in Old Shoreham Road. Some of these men had a bizarre story to tell.

It seemed a miracle had occurred during the British Army's first encounter with advancing Germans at Mons, Belgium, in August 1914. It was widely reported – and supposedly witnessed by hundreds of troops - that a vision of St George appeared in the sky accompanied by ranks of ghostly bowmen, immediately halting the Kaiser's troops. Others claimed angels descended from the heavens and threw a kind of protective shield around the British, saving them from catastrophic losses. Within weeks, across Britain, the 'Angels of Mons' had become the stuff of legend. By the end of the war it was utterly unpatriotic, treasonable even, to doubt that the claims made for it weren't hard fact.

A Scare in St Nicholas Graveyard

And all those ready to dismiss ghostly tales as sheer nonsense watch out! That's exactly the attitude of some lads who, in the early 1960s, settled themselves in St Nicholas Churchyard, at the top of North Street, for a night-time vigil, ready to dismiss tales of it being haunted. Their 'am I bothered?' attitude was soon shattered by the appearance of a hooded spectre and they were off, running down the hill screaming their heads off – very bothered indeed!

Hell-hound at Moulsecoomb Station?

Finally, coming much more up to date, a really weird occurrence of 1986, at Moulsecoomb railway station, just off the Lewes Road in Brighton and Hove. This story – reckoned to be one of the most bizarre and unexplainable occurrences of recent times - is taken from the files of the Burgess Hill group, Sussex Paranormal Investigations, and first appeared in John Rackham's amazing book, *Brighton Ghosts and Hove Hauntings*, published in 2001, and hard to get hold of now.

Two young women, who'd been for a night out, had returned home to the Moulsecoomb area, having walked all the way from central Brighton. They didn't want to go home just yet – even though it was three in the morning - so went to the station and sat in the waiting room (it's mostly an unmanned station) to chat and

Hell-hound at the station?

rest their feet. After a while, an elderly man appeared on the other side of the station and proceeded to cross the footbridge leading to the platform where the waiting room was. He was lost in the gloom for a few moments, but they waited for him to come down, fixing their gaze on the steps leading down to their side of the station. He didn't appear. There was absolutely no sign of him and he certainly hadn't retraced his steps to go back the way he'd come. They approached the bridge and went up the steps a short way, but he had completely disappeared. Puzzled and uneasy, they returned to the waiting room. What happened next was truly ghastly. A noise was heard – seemingly, at first, a couple of people larking about – but then it changed and sounded closer. Some kind of squealing, snorting animal was making for them, 'a sound close to that made by a pig, with a bleak, unearthly intensity.' The women were petrified and one struggled to put her shoes on, having slipped them off after returning from the bridge. Then, quite suddenly, there was silence. One of the women crept out to the platform. It was empty. She was about to say, 'it's gone,' or something similar, when there was a massive screeching immediately to one side of her making her flee the station via the steps down to Lewes Road. Her companion followed, but was so scared she thought she would fall and called for her friend to assist her. She, too, became aware of a presence close by and though she could see nothing, heavy breathing registered on her face accompanied by vicious grunting noises. Quaking with fear and in floods of tears, they ran for home.

Some sort of hell-hound on Moulsecoomb Station? In this day and age? All far-fetched nonsense, of course.

Remember though, as said, Brighton is one of the most haunted places in the whole United Kingdom (second only to York, it's reckoned) and in the past has been a centre for many occult practices. Until quite recently, Brighton Council even employed someone – full-time - to investigate paranormal activity in local properties.

So, maybe far-fetched nonsense - and maybe not...

And very finally...

*

Gone But Not Forgotten!

To round off this collection of bizarre Brighton bits and pieces, here's a pair of graves in the Extra Mural Cemetery, adjoining Woodvale, off Lewes Road, that just had to be included. Here lie two unrelated people buried side by side but with names that oddly connect. It's a Mr Robert Bacon buried alongside a Mrs Florence Egg!

The graves of Mr Bacon and Mrs Egg

Who said the Victorians had no sense of humour?

And who says funerals can't have their lighter side too? And what follows really did happen.

Let's say it was in 1970; a burial was to take place at Woodvale Cemetery and a grave, to the required, legal twelve feet in depth, was duly dug in preparation. But it just so happened that the 'plot' immediately next to it was also dug for another funeral, to take place at a later time. So it didn't seem like a production line in burials was taking place, this second grave was covered over with that grass-like matting you often see in greengrocers, rendering it less noticeable. However, the night before the first grave was needed it snowed, rendering the second one, under its grass-like covering, invisible!

The following day, the funeral took place, the large crowd gathering round the open grave, ready to inter the body, offer up prayers and to throw handfuls of soil down as is customary.

Once the coffin had been lowered, the priest made the sign of the cross in front of him, committed the body to the earth with full solemnity and took a few steps back with bowed head and screwed up eyes. He fell twelve feet down the second hole and disappeared in a flurry of cassock and snowflakes! Cemetery staff had to use a crane to get him out.

And in case you're wondering if the congregation laughed... They sure did!

And it's hard to follow that!

About the author

Chris Horlock was born (1953), brought up and educated in Brighton, moving to Mile Oak, Portslade in 1989, then to Shoreham, in 1996, where he lives at present. He is head of history and geography at Thomas A Becket Middle School in Tarring, Worthing, and at fifty-seven years old, thoughts of retiring and taking life a little easier are ever on his mind!

He's been married twenty years now and this is his seventh book on Brighton. Chris is also a regular writer for *Sussex Life* magazine, contributes intermittently to the *Argus* newspaper and various property magazines and continues to dash all over Sussex giving talks on Brighton's history.

He has a collection of thousands of Brighton prints, photographs, maps, plans, architect's drawings and ephemera and knew all the old Brighton historians like Antony Dale (Chris illustrated the last book he wrote) and James Gray, frequently visiting him at his home in Shirley Avenue, Hove, and swapping old photos.

If *Bizarre Brighton* goes down well, his next book could be *Bizarre Sussex*, featuring all sorts of weird and wonderful tales of the county that he's unearthed doing his *Sussex Life* articles - but with a few more Brighton tales included (of course!).

By the same author –

Brighton, The Century In Photographs I
Brighton, The Century In Photographs II
Brighton and Hove Then And Now I
Brighton and Hove Then And Now II
The Neat And Nippy Guide To Brighton's History
Brighton: The Sixties

SB Publications

For details of other fascinating books by S B Publications on East and West Sussex and other counties of south-east England, please visit our website:

www.sbpublications.co.uk

Or contact us at: 14 Bishopstone Road, Seaford, East Sussex, BN25 2UB
Tel: 01323 893498 Email: *sbpublications@tiscali.co.uk*